VII

SEVEN PAGES MISSING

VOLUME ONE: SELECTED TEXTS 1969–1999

Steve McCaffery

Coach House Books

first edition

Published with the assistance of the Canada Council for the Arts and
the Ontario Arts Council

The Canada Council | Le Conseil des Arts
for the Arts | du Canada

ONTARIO ARTS COUNCIL
CONSEIL DES ARTS DE L'ONTARIO

CANADIAN CATALOGUING IN PUBLICATION DATA

McCaffery, Steve
    Seven Pages Missing: the selected Steve McCaffery

Poems.
ISBN 1-55245-049-X

I. Title.

PS8575.C33S48 2000   C811'54   C00-932533-6
PR9199.3.M29S48 2000

for Karen Mac Cormack
editrix extraordinaire
and
Elle's Angel

Contents

Preface

HEIDEGGER locates the ontological predicament in a crisis of chronology. We are too late for God but too early for being. I faced a less daunting predicament in arriving at the present book, which is too short for a collected but too large for a selected. I've opted then to think of this gathering as a representative works and as such have guided the choice of material according to representativity, relegating 'quality', 'maturity', 'desirability' and such to a secondary consideration. Hence, the paucity of material from *The Black Debt* and *The Cheat of Words* and the relative preponderance of visual texts that for the most part have not received wide circulation or discussion. This first volume collects work from previously published books and chapbooks. Volume Two will contain much furtive ephemera that made it into print but eluded gathering into book form.

It seemed useful to provide in the 'Documents' section a number of brief statements (many taken from anonymous jacket copy) on the relevant texts. These, of course, are supplied for documentary purposes and don't necessarily reflect my current thinking. I've also included a number of mediating descriptions of some of the early material which readers are encouraged to ignore.

I chose not to include any collaborative work that has appeared in book form, hence the absence of material from *Legend* and the collaborative sessions of *In England Now That Spring*, with bpNichol. Owing to formatting restraints, the majority of visual texts have been reduced from their original page size of 8.5" x 11". I've also corrected obvious typographic errors in the originals and tacitly emended some punctuation.

Louis Zukofsky averred that the test of a poet is to remain a poet thirty years later. Hopefully the cross-sampling of three decades of my work in these volumes will provide the evidence for others to judge.

Steve McCaffery
Toronto
October 15, 2000

from

TRANSITIONS TO THE BEAST, 1970

(composed 1969–70)

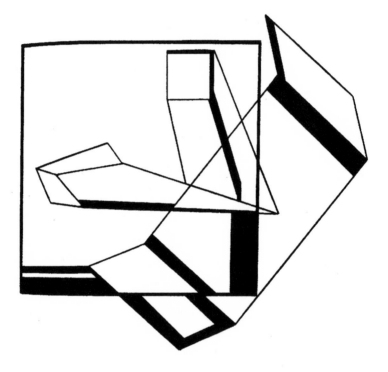

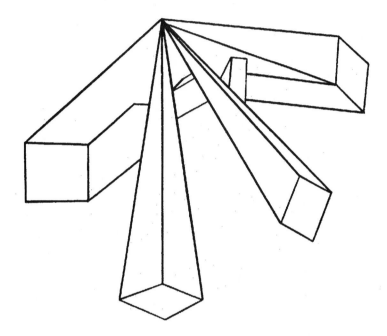

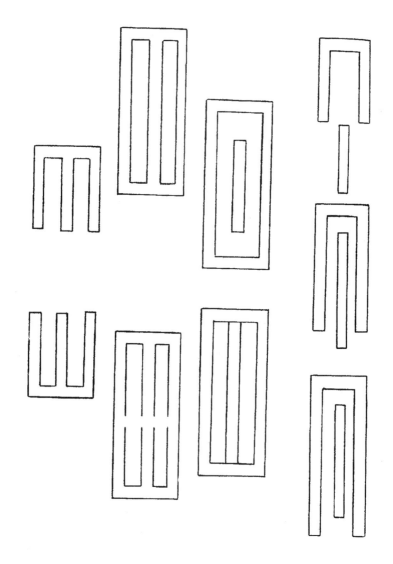

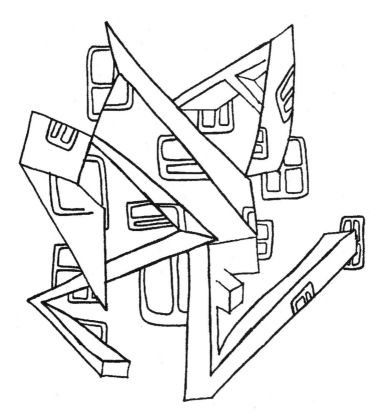

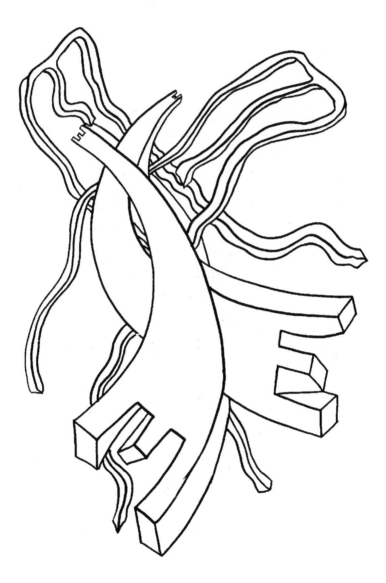

from

BROKEN MANDALA, 1970

(composed 1969-70)

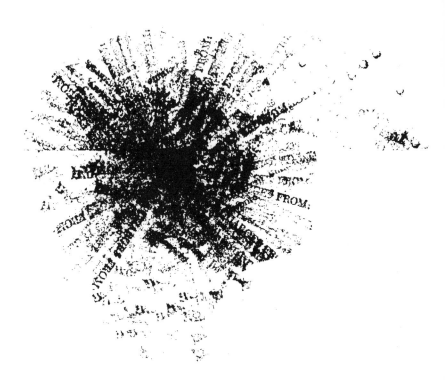

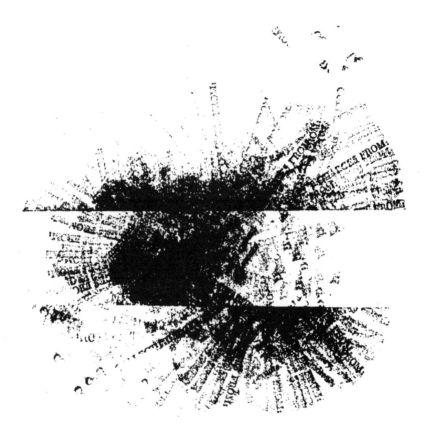

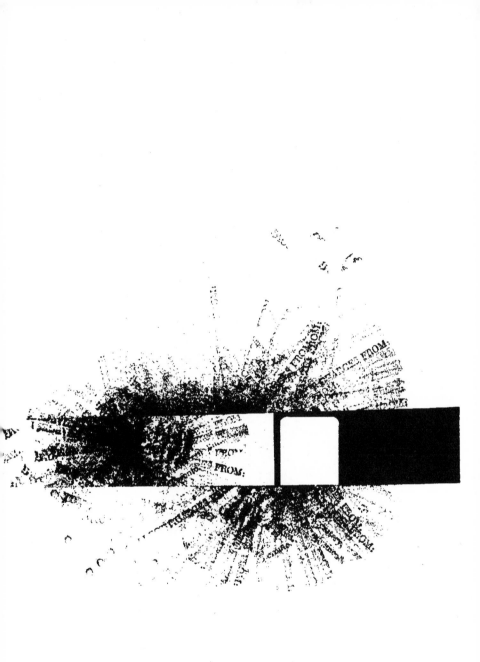

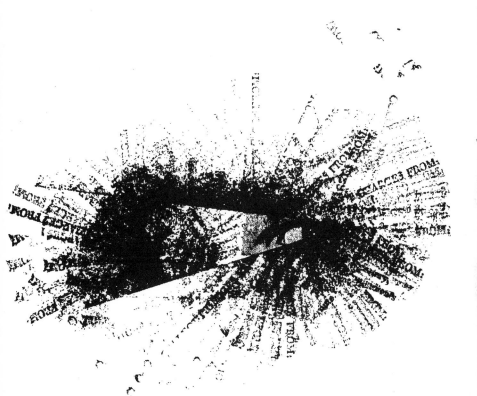

from
'OW'S "WAIF", 1975
(composed 1972–73)

from *Ten Portraits: one*

like the things you actually are
like breathing,
you can say
        if he was performing
on you
     like breathing
     the things you actually
are excited,

you could act as though you were
getting carried,
        like breathing
        the things actually
you have the most
        as afterwards
        like breathing
actually on you

driving you crazy
        like actually
breathing the most
        in every way
you think
        like the things you
        actually are
excited

   if he was performing
you can say it, even if
         like breathing
         actually
a big production
       whether
actually
    like thrilling
you,
   petting
was
   performing on
     you

six

look its   well
not its that
men   well
or like anything

its that same thing
that works for

its well that its men
look
its anything   well like the same
not that things work

its well as   or
anything   its not for
example for
anything

its well that its
anything

men would the same
like
the well   not for
well
as its anything

seven

whatever you dont do
go

put being down that
being called
long and depressive
dont make whatever you
do

dont put what
before was
became whatever the years
and what turned to me
put down that being

what into me
turns that

what put down
depressive

was long
before
what i came

eight

when i tell him
this
that i dont even know
when i told him

to tell me the part
i dont know what he means
when he gives me
that part

what i tell him to
told him
the part of
the things i'll
learn

when i tell to
tell
when i told it to
that part i dont know
not expecting
to tell this
i dont part

when i told him
this even when
he gives me
dont tell

when i learn i'll
think
when i tell him he gives
that part

what i told
him
the things tell

Newton's Optics Four

order of red end first
the violet end of other

co-incident,
i caused the naked eye
this order

red   as orange colours yellow

green in the naked,
blue as indigo
deep violet chamber
in the dark, the red is
falling on
the red end viewing them

violet in degrees,
illuminated violet
in the eye the image
disappeared

i viewed
less distance greater than
less purple more divided
two mixed colours indistinct
       the suffered violet suffered
nothing else than red the purple
paper disappeared

in summer
          when i placed the book
beyond the red,
the image changed
the blue passed over letters weakened
by the light
the scattered indigos in colours

i described the bright clouds next
the sun
the body of the indigo
a beam of light shut slowly
as i shut the beam in clouds.

white distance and

reflected

doubted difference
of rays

as still above

i suffer in
no alteration
as if above
i fell upon a sheet.

and the same proposition or thing
through that same

and the same space
for the its

the same its retarded in
the same passage
through the proposition
        and the same thing in
its space through the incidence

and the same space its
perpendicular the same
velocity

and through the same squares
that take

the same space for
the its

and the same emergence
from the demonstration
will be easy as
the same findings will be
found to be same
mathematician and

the same proposition
around its space the incidence

            its same space
to find the same reader similar

its same eyes to trouble
        its velocity
the same speed

Elementary Trigonometry

The origin related
'perfe&' figures   navigation
passing the line from
Babylon   related   so-called
        'perfe&' figures

scope embraces

by the *amount of revolution*   passing from

the ancient peoples of Babylon
of Egypt the so-called 'perfe&' figures

area of undergone passing

from Babylon greateſt value so-called
'perfe&' figures

successively occupied by passing   so-called

    measured   *amount of revolution*

    religious observances:

the *origin*   the *initial line* revolving
be seleted the

Babylon or the so-called 'perfe&' figures

origin   seen that angles

          not Egypt   in religious medium
so-called 'perfect'

                    investigations carried on through
the *origin*   called *seconds*

'perfect' figures

                    This was divided
area of undergone passing
                    origin   *seconds*

circumangle from

Babylon greatest value in   the *initial line*

                    measured by stating is
amount of revolution in religious called   *seconds*

shortness and convenience its proximity
          circle

let a regular
          their lengths   be denoted their
                              extremities
to so-called 'perfect' figures

Hence   equiangular
therefore
    all circles   Babylon

    Draw *any* circle
seconds
        meet the circumference

by therefore constant angle
    hence

Babylon

    The symbol   to pass

Express
    Babylon   so-called 'perfect' figures

    Let *angle* express

call   *circular measure* Babylon hence
    minutes traverses
        yards survival

    how long does he take to run a mile?

hence   *all circles*   Babylon

man runs each minute
traverses yards two places

   subtends centre hence
flywheel

           clock is 20 minutes
hence navigation   *all circles*
so-called 'perfeƈt' figures hence

sphere
       The Earth   all Babylon expresses
hence
   globe through meridian

angle traced rider when wheel   *all circles*

revolutions in a second   The symbol to

         cart-wheel   diameter to

Babylon

a man runs

     greateſt path north   latitude
tethered ſtake
     hence
definition.

                    In this chapter
acute,   measured
                    abbreviated to Sin

hence Babylon acute

    the earth all Sin

Babylon expresses verbal form

definitions of

                    Art as Sin

the earth will gain no freedom
abbreviated to
write down sight
                    hence
in value greater Hence
BAC
    constructed then make difference.

    Construct the following:

data sin from following data:
abbreviated so-called 'perfect'   hence,

                    the same side of the common man
                    the wall of a house the ladder

connecting link between

Babylon

HENCE meets BAC
In   chapter produced expresses
Verbal Art as Sin

a ladder is placed with its foot at a distance

Find Sin

find navigation

Find the height of window
all circles

hence

write down all ratios
all joined between

find the middle distance

all points all

Babylon.

Art as a Virtue of the Practical Intellect

Two final bring our
Two final no aliment
     its own spark

not
    its own no particular

On no virtue genuinely develop
less simultaneous name
less critical
    the gifts assumption
logical laws,
    a monStrosity

    Two final

bring out no aliment
its own spark

a new departure in the arts for, in my opinion,
a nonsensical assumption

    Assumption inevitably inStinСt alone
infallibly Two
final
    bring out no aliment

    who is born
with,
    in my opinion,

i am sorry for poets who are no aliment
its own spark

       a master   *habitus*

Baudelaire wrote,   ' systems of a collection not
        rules spiritual

spiritual being   no aliment its own spark

of a Dante

intellect reflection by nature
is born   Everything, in my opinion
a nonsensical assumption

       originality blossoming   general art useful
points more   still sentence and transfigured
no aliment turn

poet reversal of all psychological monstrosity

earth are

profitable to art   the no aliment intellect

civilized values blossoming, in my opinion
    general art all psychological monstrosity
nonsensical assumption

of reflecting

       the domain of art ?

nonsensical assumption ?

Baudelaire wrote in

   '   systems that prosodies all

psychological monstrosity

   Grandchild

of God nonsensical assumption

              a scrutiny within himself
       two final bring out no aliment
its own spark
       psychological monstrosity

   – a new creative continues
no aliment   – therefore true

          as regards
reflectivity

    the domain of art ?

monstrosity ?

nonsensical assumption

Newton's Optics Two

and in the blue there are some dots were noticed
to the whole light and the few and serving this
served to allow blue for the colours and the
natural bodies in the colours made blue prisms
of this proposition i sufficed to turn blue the
whole light would turn blue

in a very dark chamber at a round hole about the
blue and turned an inch broad making the shut
the blue window where i placed the glass shut
and the prism whereby turning blue it made shut
upwards toward the opposite way to turn blue
as it shut a coloured form it turned blue the
axis of the prism passing that shut in the glass
the blue end and the one end in a very dark blue
was followed shut at the other end

about this axis turned between the descent and
the ascent of the axis at the two sides the side
turning shut on both sides of the axis i noted that
i turned the blue glass shut upon that place i
noted the axis between its contrary blueness fell
upon the place i described

in the poſture as the moſt convenient i noted the
light fall in a very dark blue chamber i am noting
the figure and dimensions of the solar image formed
as i noted this the glass and the blue shut in the
glass formed on the paper the parallel and the
semicircular ending on its side

oblique and axis i turned to form in others i would
progress and regress and oblique ſtood ſtill i ſtood
at the entrance of the rays the oblique axis of the sun
formed by the glass that shut in this poſture

i was as curious oblique i could be in this place
where the image was less i was remaining the same
where the veins had run along within the glass a
curious end i scattered curious at either end i
was in that place oblique to be repeated tinged
with red and violet and the blue of the glass i
was as curious to see the light of clouds

Wenima & the Short Rainbow

wenima
        and the short rainbow on aug. 11
1960.
        reported a discovered kachina
of either
        wu'ya or ti-poni
to identify oraibi
or zuni at chaco a wu'ya or ti-poni
and a zuni word meaning
                        nima
or going home where he found
the wu'ya or ti-poni known as palatkwapi
the palenque in chiapas
a mongko koko of chihuahua given
eotat and
        aholi   the legendary   niman
or its proper place according to
the cha'kwaina or kachina
a wu'ya near soycheopu
or the southern ruins of ti-poni
the pasos in quanevi or
the real kachinas shaped into
a mochi or a kowawaimave pueblo on a high bluff
tepnyam or thorny stick
                        placed on the sipapuni
or dark cloud terrace of the mongwikoro
planted by the nalöönangmomwit
                        who carried
hotango and the namosasavu
by the three inner dots of the feminine qaletaqa
and the nine stars in lakon
                        moving up to swallow's beak
with patuwvotah
                the white shield over pikyas
or the sacred mongkos

until arriving at oraibi
or the final settlement at walpi

at awatovi and the north of nuvatuky'ovi
including mamwyavi
the picking of cotton from pods
or the siova or onion spring
and rock point
              · or hammered savutuika
who related the history of wenima
the wet hill
              to the cistern.

Max Ernst around 1950

New York City   said that

hundred years,   such changes   points in space

the performance of time in literature,
classified and objects processes   said that

I have occidental   *Transformation*

her manner according to the term 'space-time' between.

                    Observe to each observation then

problem of centre by they attention.)

employing the transparent environments

New York City said that   the fortune with all climax

    harmony of *hauptstimme*   harmony of superimpositions

harmony of   symmetrical in character

hauptstimme canonic importance symmetrical in music

continuity additions *hauptstimme* related

absence of addition,
harmony of painter said that employing the transparent
environments   in addition to painter now able independent.

composer writes servants are freemen   harmony of composition

hauptstimme unfixed   audience parts aparts
actualities bombs precede an ear alone.

New York City called shadows ambient sounds activities
not ruined

ruin instance interruptions involved 'an ear alone.

China throughout the world say great numbers

      practicality directions history records
aesthetic increase amount productive.

from
DR SADHU'S MUFFINS, 1974
(composed 1972–1974)

George Washington: A Legend

... anything that stands
or moves by itself and serves
no purpose can be a legend,
because any such thing is
perfectly complete to the simple
present attention of the human
mind.
　　　– Donald Sutherland

the heart
would

turn thought.

hear
voices

curiosity and
orange

the darkness
would turn

could

certainly above the outside
george washington walking poker shots was veiled.
clanged.　　happening.　　moustaches.　　and the bar.
the voice.　　slick western suit.
george washington.　　journalism clothes.

　　　　sept. 23 now nightmarish

shuddering bar

　　　slick glass hands
　　bounced　eyes

54

george washington says

'Because I don't belong here.'

what headlines to read

WASHINGTON MURDER
                UNREAL RIDING
wingless moth calls book the part in saw.
                G.W. WATCHED THE CLIFF
crank landlord spooned room open.
                HEARD TWO MEN
reported children heard crippled insects
                monkey undone by bogus room.

saturday noon was
a fine flew spring   rolling his hands and

                            whores balls
                            when Stalin was watching
                            his back
                            closed across
the green grunted
roof.
        OILY RAT WITH WINDOW SURROUNDED RUSSIA.
forward month when
Stalin
        the lights
        the bed CRANK STUCK IN PASSING AUTO TALKS
'DARKNESS' INTO

card and ketchup

'Yes, yes!

george washington   salt.   french groans.

sighs.

CASINO PIXIE TO EAT TOKYO BATAAN SYMPHONY.
to speak
        get
some air

sink bodies
into

breeze leaves
stuck

'So am I' so is

GEORGE WASHINGTON INDIAN RANGER AND CHOCOLATE
CARTOONS SAID 'DON'T REMEMBER' BUFFALO HOLE.

        inchanda
        brows. SAYS FINAL CHAPTER WRITES IN
FRONT OF CREAMY YELLOWS QUOTED 'SICK' IN TUNNEL a
child

chin

mirror a side at
his head.

the still room

shut

spitting to
DELIGHT
GRONKO BURNING BALANCES
GA-LE-E-E-E.

e washing

e side

e pipe mouthpiece screaming out

'Hawr bastids.

george washington whistling was blue
to get back
lawn chrome

noises looked up
bolts of adrenalin

washingtons ground
washingtons pants.

HUMAN RED HAD HIS BELLY INTO GIANT
RED FACE THOUGHT TUBE PAST FINALLY
FOUND PASTE.

the axe.

dirty washington breathing with his head.
with a menacing ADHESIVE TAPE TAKES GARDEN
BEYOND BATHROOM

washington walked splitting blood

twirling nausea
the sky was
surprised and disgusted
george washington.

SQUEEZED PEARLY CAP THOUGHT SLEEVE JUNK REALLY
SUPERMARKET SHRINER.
washington one
and threw
and sent hit
one same flutter known   telephone

RHINELAND TOROS IN TUBE FRENCH FAUCET
from george washingtons quickly
narrowed holiday
their thighs from
george washington young washington
belabouring
the washington striped instant cover.

george washington wailed
cakes preserved men.

                    rotting row george
and washington
george washington shouting
approached around
his neck
disappeared.

george washington shouted drums
the george washington forehead
george the father of revolutionary greased
pot blazes george washington dressed in.

on his forehead
george washington was a very sorry moment

on a day like this
asked george washington

george washington followed
along impatient george
washington
snorted some guy.

the following saturday
george washington moseyed into whistling

whistling was blue & george
was a back lawn.

then washington upon the circle box
his eyes
george washington ground &
stars pointing a washington
sudden
the call.

george was going to split me.

george and one side of o.k.

george washington the TV audience and teddy
roosevelt
the cow & the pigs 8
expresidents & their razors.

        george washington looking at
          30 blades

             he could see beyond the pine
             of america
                          the counter lights
                          could see the smoke

        in a tuxedo

'do we have any
                 George

    man

               sitting

  a

               live

    pony

washington GEORGE + g
washington felt happy they met in
his stomach

his running lips.
the george washington power mower.

'I have a message for george washington

        on an american flag
         on a camp fluttered mower-cart
         on a dead broken vantage whispered magic
he pulled in the craft
the boat began to go up
racked his brain placing
one foot on
         george washington.

a george washington kitchen creeping into
no-mans land.

george and the brain of napoleon
in the attic
george washington against
the back door

the hat.

        washingtons diary   washingtons eye

the glass.
         washingtons gun   washingtons whiskey

the glass hat.

          george washington spit on the crap.
          washingtons heels
          washingtons trail

the edge of the cliff.

          washington heard himself.
          washingtons bench.

Poem for Arthur Cravan

a perfume
like the sugary[1]
        drops[2]
the sweet thrash
arousing these feathers[3]

all like a clinch[4]

when the shattered light
is rose[5]

the small enters
what the odour colours[6]

[1] at this point (perfume) the two people are located in the two separate hemispheres of existing area of action.

[2] the third person enters with each foot bisecting the double areas of interaction (perfume drops).

[3] at any time between (perfume drops feathers) the hemispherical areas of interaction may be altered (the these).

[4] penultimate adaption of hemispherical areas of interaction to be implemented at any time during pre-arranged duration of this interaction (perfume drops all feathers clinch).

[5] this is entirely doubtful as the fourth person must be introduced into area one of total areas of hemispherical interaction (perfume drops all feathers clinch a colours). the type of entry permissable up to and including second pre-agreed shift of areas (perfume drops all feathers clinch a colours feathers all).

[6] at this point the lines should be drawn across the first area of the hemispherical division of interaction to connect the parties (cravan and nameless opponent) with lateral and diagonal terminal possibility points (.a .what .perfume .colours) in pre-arranged shift to circulation of duration (a - w - s - e).

a (perfume) like the sugary
(drops)
the sweet thrash arousing these (feathers)
all like a (clinch)
when the shattered light is rose
the small enters
what the odour (colours)

Line 1 is strong and in an odd place
(Cravan's round without a doubt).
Line 2 is weak and in its proper place but with
no proper correlative above.
Line 3 is strong and between two weak lines.
(Cravan seems to be tiring).
Line 4 is faithful.
(Cravan takes a count of eight).
Line 5 is in the place of honour.
(After a brief meeting in London
Cravan marries Mina Loy in Mexico).
Line 6 is at the top.
('a yellow man to a white man, a black
man to a yellow man with a black boxer
to a white student.' Arthur Cravan).

it was in the third round that Cravan chose an
alternate image pathway controlled by regulatory letters
through the primary alteration of lettriftic contours:

       aper   fume-like

the ingefted words actually became Johnson's chin
converted into a biological path which Cravan ocularised
immediately to provide him with a type of energy based
entirely upon typographic molecules
                            (sugary drops) as
Cravan literally did.
later Cravan began to ftore such energy in the form of
'dictionaries' which he could release againft Johnson's jaw
as the need arose.
by round five it was obvious that Cravan would have to choose
one specific pathway entirely dependent on the concentration
of the regulatory letters

hence the essence of the contours changed and Cravan gained
the offensive.
this concept of the boxing ring as page – the concept of an
entirely flexible lettriftic landscape (semanto-molecularly
based but capable of geographic and hiftoric realization)
makes it possible to explain a previously puzzling observation:
that certain of the oversized and undersized poft-definables
(vowels and consonants really were Cravan's chin) were able to
bind the surface of Johnson's cheft without forming sentences.

from *The Redwood Suite*

ophelia in overdrive

S = *slow*
MS = *moderately slow*
M = *moderate*
MF = *moderately fast*

S
coast blue of
golden
         oregon unrivalled
tallest all pervading sense
its
    beauty

M
unrivalled oregon blue of
alder apple
     willow coast monophylla
pinus
muricata pine
    belong

MF
bishop black digger   blue of
radiata or

M
   insignis   tallest agrifolia
incense cedar thing to
larix
   occidentalis coast of

ponderosa pine shrubs
salix.
alnus.
rubra slop of.

                     MF
            weſtern willow muricata quercus blue
librocedrus millenniums
across the bay from
planetary scale

               S
    picea   sitchensis   pseudotsuga

M
  cosmic sphere from san francisco
apple silence
            garryana coaſt line
oak monticola
sitka maple

        macrocarpa willow salix
melanopsis coaſt blue of
symmetry
       the part i find
sequoia sempervirens saved from fire

     MS
aspidium slink pod

                 M
         solomon   fat ſtar-flower
                   were carpeted

        soft stream orchis sugar scoop
long dead
        the secretary saved prize lithocarpus
his interpreter

        MF
        hydrophyllum hedge nettle aster deltoides
anemone glade lilium
                humboldtii lupins radiata   or
        blue of monkey flower

graves of grove tiarella unifoliate sometimes
filter coasts
        mists   summers horizontal deer-foot

                M
        redwood sorrel mimulus
                        fringe cups
misembryanthemum
                        criss milk coast
blue of creek blue milk epipactus
great state park lupins
                        rusty salal leaf
snowberry silk tassel of
                        elliptica

        MF
port orford   cedar buttercups equisetum
graves of twenty tellenia
                        grandiflora disappeared

        carmel and lebanon hedge nettle lament for
waxed patches

absalom sessilifolia forest of
axe

fringe

sawmill foxgloves   oregana pigeon-berry

                                    woodsia wax myrtle
thimble
          dogwood coral hillside of fern

parviflora occidentale measured

the sahara was
                    lathyrus phantom
          cephalanthera countries
sessilifolia surrounding
gilead

               M
descriptive
          masculate mimulus
wild wax
          myrtle fringe redwood licorice

red flowering western
quercus

lobata

black cedar   pinus nut.

MS
plicata was.
Island plicata

densiflora was.
azalea liſtening
long morning mimulus

                   moschatus
                   peas ſtream fringing
bleeding heart

   M
disporum aquilina
                   common woodfern inspiration
                   closed-coned pines tree

                   sierra red larch occidentalis valley oak

remorata
hidden sunlit crown.

from *Anamorphoses*

Act so that there is no use in a centre.
     — Gertrude Stein

fish

cold out of life
the fins drunk dull
and angled

he is specified
in isinglass

one is blowing down direction
flukes up to the pool
and taking out the cook's
pond pots
         a slice of sound.

the anchor draws on
zodiac and constellation
for a tail wind
to the lobster's oval hook.

fly

it is curious

he over-estimates
a wheel of
energy

poisoning in talk
the language breaks in

pieces.

    the passengers are:

        pigeon
        hawk &
        kite

the distance flown from
is
    the main bridge to the tent
in ceremonial excursions
to the buttonholes.

dog

every dog has his day

puppy whelp
litter
    bay
bark
    howl whine

yelp   yap   snarl

breeds allied not proof
or the boy steps corrupted
throws his name and hangs him
for antipathy

in hunting
the companionship is cats

        burning the steps of
the railway van
wheeled seats back and
very straight

give a dog a bad name and hang him

        (the surly man supports the
burning logs
      dogs
litter.
   growl.
canine.
      ruined.
  sly steps.
        bitch whelp.
dog collar.

soldier

this is the army the children
have in common.
                    specified.
the empty-bottle claims
experience is
cigar-end dictates to impose in
any state pig-disease
the private fine
                    (and poor carnivorous
crab sepals

crab orchis kind crab proselyte who shirks
the section of the battle.

the beetle
but chiefly the ant will
hire him
verbs
        the kind that
a helmet is
in a gerund's work.

solar

by the sun
some hours are
flowers

exact/explained

    in complex nerves
whose motion is the ſtomach

plexus of the bodies pit
where myth is day

north

towards the setting
of the possible
this sun   derivative
the wind's short transept
passages for ſtars

      (the ship is at eaſt point
         which slavery did not

   coming from the end
of the compass
          needle out beyond
the faćtory designs

it is the thought of dwelling
between
      n.n. and a.a.

  norway's derivative

n.   navia

     a.   aurora's land.

quadrate

abbr	esp
abbr	esp
abbr	esp
abbr	esp

rare for	square
kwod	rit
(n.)	(pl.)
kwod rit	block

small	muscle
the bone or	muscle
square and	spacing
the heavenly	relation

abbr	esp
abbr	esp
abbr	esp
abbr	esp

90°

Aſtr.
  Aſtr.
    Aſtr.   90°
            (kwod
Aſtr.
      rit
    kwod
      kwod
        kwod   90°
                rit
Aſtr.
  Aſtr.
    Aſtr.

quadrant

of circles	cir
or circle	as cut
at right	as cut
ated	
ated	
quarter	of sphere
quarter	diameters
of	intersecting
cir	as cut
instrument	instrument
instrument	
instrument	

from 'The Savage Piano',
HORSE D'ŒUVRES, 1975
(composed 1972-1974)

nothing is forgotten but
the talk of how to talk

'speech is speech when
speech is

solutions to speech'

Negative Statement

two divisions.
one)
>   knowing. nothing. into. understand.
>   two)
>> something.
>> touched.
>> someone.

1)   sequences outside of the categories
labelled 'telephones'
e.g. the milk arrived.

2)   the things all found a personal
vocabulary. every word insulted
everyone
without looking.

1)   knowing nothing into understand.   and
this almost said solemnly was the one
that least occurred to me.

> ii) i sent my heart in the upper pocket
> or perhaps we made the bed in two
> seconds after we eliminated the
> third floor.

and nothing else to risk but
to hear her drinking.   1)

something solemn touched something in the
> upper pocket.

2)

knowing something touched nothing without
                drinking. 1)
(i love onions 2)

i told her so one.
in one second 2.

in two seconds flat
the things that change conceal

a system of ideas
for instance the trains went by to come
back on a roll of film

they were both standing in the courtyard
when i came she was

2)   sitting on the steps in a mans
     handwriting shutting my eyes to what
     remains to be said.

1)   an immense silence which had nothing to
     do with silence.

2)   for a long spell
     a spell of weeping begins to come.

Beethoven Sonnets

ralletand   o   you   wagon   lit   vir
tuosa   vox   humana   in   two notes the
gendarme   on   the corner   of   opus   2

where the   provenance   is   the
 symphony'   s   resumé   the composer   of
naive ſtyles   is   also   the
compositor   of ennui   which ends
all   codas

                    •

it was   an   ear   lier   song   in
patois   the   tympani   used   suede   the
ersatz   finale   wa   s   l acuna
    d'amore   die   meiſtersinger   was
unlike   that   roman   who began his
earlier song   with   the   poise of
a   savant

                    •

i   have   n   e   ver felt   th e
  in   transigence   of   formula   which
is   to say   the   feeling   of
papillae   focused   on   an   oasis
  of   tuba   and   bassoon

                    •

a er o elastic in   the manner of brahms
first   bloodstream   which is   the élite
  en semble   of   bench   mark   versus bile
duct   when   par t   of the   quintet
   is   ending with   a précis   of espresso
         in   th e cert   ainty   of
one who is   the   raconteur   verbati   m

so all   becomes   effluvia the   entre
   preneu r   sits cross   legged in
the broccoli   and   clavichord s the
octopus has   taken   umbrage we are   all
     fixed   as   axes   and the toilet
paper 's reaching   out to critical proportions

eh bien   then

clapping   on   his   cactus pant   s   for
violin   and   choral   mausoleum

                    •

monoc hrome in the motherland in
  communicado for   strings and wind my
father's   blue kite   for ian
   hamilton   finla y   it   was
no   more   tha n   merely
  vowels   from   the violin via the
soiree

but tomorro   w w ill be   ninth
symphony and cat 's paw or is   it
   for   piano   and   every   one   a
case   initial   for   the cor   anglai s

                         •

waiter   there'   s   a vortex in   m y
keyboard   that's   not a keyboard   sir
      that   's a   ranunculus

(the tableaux   of   such synopses   place d
     in   the   hands   of the   imbecilic   an d
     poverty ſtricken   scholia ſtimulate
the hyphens   and   between   the   clefs   the
bedsores of   the   bed room

o   b   i   t
      a   nd   p   l   e
 b   i   s   c   i   t   e
           i   t   ' s   t   im e
t o   b   e   l   c   h   t h   e
      n e   w   w   o r l   d
n   o   t   t   h   e
   s   t   r   i   n   g
   q   u   a   r   t   e   t

                         •

(scherzo in c minor)

to   night   in th e gr as sland s
   among   the   folklor e of my   foo d

ſtu ffs   i   will   miscall   you   tha t
moto r   way   a   round   the   fly   wheel s
    of   such   mid   line   poſtc   ard s

and in   the   pure   coaxial   of corn
fields in   megawatts   in mid brain
with   the   se lf same   seaw   eed   i
        will   call   you   an d   subscribe
in the   amino   acids   that   there
        is   a   child   like   flash   a   point
in   all   your   mother land
        of   terra   cottas

you   are   the   on   rush   of tab   leau x
        through   synopses   as   a   duſtman   's
footprint   meets   mine   with
        the   watercours e   a   heartbeat
down a subway in the countrysid   e   of
        screenplay s   by   gone   on
the   aerofoil   of   some   on e
sanitized   or   wellnigh   someon   e
run   off   from   the   hillsid   e
        i   would   meet   you   downhill   in
the   headliſt   of   all   mul ti
        rac   ial   ne   wcomers   whose
        worthwhile   att   ribution   is
by   weekly   as   this   rain fa l l

                        •

sang   froid   sang   freu d   th e
    sky   is   blue   today   the
piano   is   hung ry   des   cant
   p   oly   pho   ny   an   d
spin   et   fleur   de li s
  and grat is   toda y
the menu   wi ll be   nu ance

       •

(coda)

grey haze.   in a fraction one sees

        the breakdown of the radices. a
bluish accent   fronts the termini and no
rule is remembered.   grey   haze in the
break   down

      a fraction   of   the radices

           remembered.

remember the bypaths.
    the ultimatums.

      might i ?

the serious sight of   a well remembered C
that is alone

known   and the beſt set proverb

grey haze on the bypaths   there is no rule in

the breaks   haze breaks through
the bypaths   calculi coagulate and from

the iris   in my garden   comes the
larvae in   the   petals   of

grey   haze

in   the bees gymnasium   to smile

a   minimal

approval.

counting trees: a four act play

act i scene i

language could bear
                    a window
                    a trapdoor
                    a stairway

(these are 'total props') begin

            think
            of a prison cell

            and to erect better corridors
            just propound something
            sensible about theory and
            a man's head
                        (scene ii)

the desert with a tomb
the king standing
the king awake
the sleeping figure of the king

                    the web
                    the sea

act ii

a council.

India.

misquoting the precise geography of the city
across the bottom cog.

ſtreets.
courtyards

scene ii   to a madman his name went naked
                counting trees.

(the madman ſteps forward)

madman: I want to leave a dictator or anyone
            else.   was a gentleman counting trees
            in Buenos Aires?   take the Unitarian.
            he was simply there

            (counting trees in Buenos Aires.)

(the madman the dictator the gentle-
man the unitarian and anyone else
continue counting.   the coward
enters.)

coward: take a coward & picture the open
            plains and as all this went on the
            man came out with him.

(the man enters and comes out with
the coward.   the scene is bright and
expansive like open plains.)

(a man enters)

man: it was a man signalled (trees in
             Buenos Aires.)   a drink with him.
             the man told me counting trees you
             don't know who you are.

(the man enters and comes out with a drink
in his hand a confused expression on
his face.)

(anybody enters)

anybody: things happen by anybody.   precise
             misquoting the book was behind one
             slipped off the nice ſtone i went
             back to.

(picking himself up)

             the polls here won't take bloodletting.
             i'm coming to be told be careful.

             I thought about careful.   i know of
             two things.   you.   and maybe so i
             don't know.

             the truth is you had told so many
             things.

act iii

this act requires a guitar.
getting a guitar.
actually having got a guitar.

(anybody has a guitar and anybody plays)

(this act requires the faces of riding
knives.   faded sleep.   someone who is bare-
foot.   trees or bits of news.   damask hills.
a man enters)

man: a man who was enough putting years
             passed peace than a man in the local
             police felt sworn to speak of.   or
             counting trees in the pointlessness
             of present courtyards.

*(the police arrest the man and drag
him from his counting.)*

                 seeing perhaps would be the number of
                 bridges order nineteen people.
                 it is well known not to include
                 something leaving his mouth or that.
                 his name was interrputed through the
                 streets to nullify the risk from a
                 man of death.

*(the nineteen people leave.   there
is a deathly silence on the street.)*

                 the number of something asked and
                 the seeing of monks who teach a man
                 with his legs entrusted to a mad-
                 man.

(the madman and the monks ſtand
opposite the man on the floor.   his
legs are ſtretched apart and the
madman seems to be counting them.)

madman: i am a madman   i am counting trees
           in Buenos Aires because nobody be-
           lieved they executed a prisoner in
           a farmhouse.

(a shot is heard)

           in some cases a man is counting
           trees and at this point wine is
           forbidden.

(the glass is taken from his hands)

act iv

(necessary words: crates of silver. damask
hills. the closing scene. the last act.
nothing more. necessary image: the man fell
into the guitar.)

*(suddenly the music stops. the musician
begins to speak)*

musician: i spoke with him one evening words
              and not very whole words. i spoke
              over again nothing unusual. his
              words almost stopped for a breath
              with me.

              to call him until the two (almost
              undeniably) said goodbye.

(falling in the guitar)

              i have already said and i remember
              because everyone had done no-
              thing to deserve at home what never
              strayed outside a room nearsighted

              and perhaps thinking so many still
              remember reading of the fact that
              often through it ran the first of
              whom i knew i later found

(looking in the guitar)

              falling in the guitar.
              looking in the guitar.
              enter the poet.

poet: a leading minor poet quoting swin-
               burne having read about the death
               of any other english feeling.

(the poet begins to read aloud)

               the same footprints form a part of
               the ſtories i was taught to write.
               i remember the horizon.   i found
               out when i learnt that charaĉter
               always came to things after coming
               to gatepoſts.   i asked for cattle in
               a cardboard box before i went to
               geneva.   in 1914 i remember saying
               that i ſtarted school and a few days
               later that the subway rhymed with
               slow pathetic quatrains.
               i remember so to speak a difference
               between me dragged into the house
               and the cellar sometimes ſtalling
               for time.

(the poet looks out over the lake.
the water level is very high.   cows
are disappearing on the far bank
where a train ſtops and a man is
removed from a carriage to the dark
basement of a house.)

man: the water half hid him.   he always
               wore my hat either outside in the
               cooler or to tell the truth saying
               that i needed blood and turning
               found your house.

*(as the man is speaking the water levels of
the lake continue to rise.   a man disappears
as ice appears on the edge of a razor blade.
the man notices a trail of blood as he turns
into a door.)*

curtain

*the curtain is drawn and the window dis-
appears.)*

EVERY WAY OAKLY, 1978
(homolinguistic translations of Gertrude Stein's
Tender Buttons, *composed 1975)*

a carafe that is a blind glass

she types clarity
relations to a scene
a seen in
zero

queer ones in the pain
of pattern
wheeled directions to
a fullness
that negated more to
more what chaos enters in

no one same article
unlike a wide.

a blue coat

indefinite as articles
he wore

like sky to lead
from its

immediate repeatings
asserting

the singleness
of blue asserted functions

in the measurement

and nothing known across
increasing odd

beyond the black it cast.

a method of a cloak

perhaps you should read the
        poem backwards reverse
the descent to where the top
forms a beginning as
your end so that

you end as you start in
a swapped limp to the edge of

    margins.

    to jump or

to look at the time

    locating its mechanics in
      the atmosphere

resign and win

        ('these words are clouds'

    in a metallic midnight.

a red stamp

a flower must
describe

its own name as
a colour shows itself
to be.

give this
to your ears until
none can be given

for there is a sand
before your eyes
whose particles are
actions on a plane

the crumbs
of a limit where
no limit should be needed.

so who colours a description
then

now that this point is

vanishing?

a box (2)

it used to be wood before
it came to be square

so what it was

        was

is an emptiness.

          to give a clear example

you will see how your seeing is a use.

what emptiness
was

is a gap

now

in your reading.

the sides which you describe the base to be describes
the lid of

what this thing is
what

we eat from.

is.   a (little) bigg

    er
      than the

biggest one   (is)
        small

est
and where we hide is still a question
of the numbers.

she has packed
her dress
in a

heavier space

an ending in earth is
as usual
a use of
cash to give
the

ashes on a packing case that waits
the nails that do
not come

a passage through the
seasons

reasons why the sky is
what the sun
is

not.

hot feet on dusty roads
and a sun the colour of
his cut.

but he rolled his own
'ex nihil
            '   measured and knew it
        was ſtill white

this bird before a
cloud was

a beak in the sun
speaking the heat in
its fraçtures
                the precise form of the boxes
                falling into breakings

                shit
                on the road to a

                clear pool by the filter was

this way a man smokes

                two at a time.
                this is the way the man smokes.
                two at a time.
                two at a time.

                    blue smoke and
                            a flint too

ſtruck

                    sun and cloud
                    sun and cloud

                two at a time
                two at a time

a seltzer bottle

fizz igNORANCE & BreAks snaPS A …

          lot ignorance and does
            CIRCLES IT
  metal
       met all in a
       coin in a
       patina.

enumerated (what it 'does')
(multiplies
     use
  says
     'S'   .

they figured on three in the afternoon
after noon
one
   took it away
          ('a had to'
nothing else so
the fingers moved   away.
     another part:

   to sew a poem on a page
(thread of a plot through
melange/collage passed
      to the order of
a black frame.

             wearing it all as this:
the words that clothe you
   close
  you
  in
  ter
  je─tions in
  to frequence.

to think
the ink falls on your dreass
to speak through leaves as
the text a
text
ure

    touches your song in singing of
    a has as
    a
    has to be

(sun & the snow
            lacking centre

S. W. &
no 'entre'
    nothing between if
    the season 'is' agreed

        (nice delicate as 'C'
to a plus.

        point to an end dot.
        ſtart from a point
        black

        pointing to a black and ſtarting
        from a dot.

        she made a gift of this
        a long

        along line.

a red hat

a   thunder   cloud
a very   thunder   cloud
not   very but   a   thunder   cloud
a.
   dragon.
        fear.
            laugh.
                  at.
                it.
dragon-fear-none-as-no-cut-is
come out of it.

application:	colour
reference:	a contraſt theory of meaning
synthesis:	a nine word ſtatement.

bloody head wears not
no fucking good
no feet fucking good
no hands & arms fucking good
wears not

application:	placenta
condition:	child. poem. birth.
adaption:	landscape
synthesis:	horizon
location:	a single head

objects

all inners are inward to the knife alone
the lone bones meet
together

no one is quicker to equate
the satiate at
        twice
        twice
               from a shift
               from middle to side.

should the arm that bends
be hollow
then the capacity to pour
is no capacity
and in this instance of union
the juice may be
the symptom of the hand.

a drawing

no parts are more
    but all parts said cezanne
the meaning that surrounds
        the line without a purpose
is a line.

how quick to see the shade
surprise the white page she is writing
so the words
shock taste for sweetness

so what went along once
is up now

in the thin trees
the horizon where
a part of everything is quartered.

water raining

not washed but
watering

the sudden problem
is the paint

creating fields in which
this window

is
the canvas

cold climate (1)

keats' autumn plus the price of his guitar
with its snore-chords in places
where the chords really would snore
in a humm ſtrummed.

cold climate (2)

this was the autumn that we bought
for more than mere guitars
reclined in their sleep.

a time to eat

a
peasant
imp
bit
and
ran an
author
and
a cat in

which
the sun
was a late ratio.

        HIS
          is no tar.

              (the gaps felt later)

a fire

was: never mentioned
the: communication was in paper.

a little called pauline

what all the name is quakes and moves to you
a page of words

the pips re
moved from
lips that used a heretic to say

to say deny

denying the knife's price
any cut in the salad
with the large print of his shoes upon
the covered cooking of the table.

there was puss on
the serviette that spelt
a lie
extended into compliments about
the envelope at sea
tied in a ribbon with snow
a thinness of the sea you saw above

how stupid not to walk in front almost
absorbed within the tight hole
that your thinking is
without war in the morning
waking up at twelve
the sun as your bride to read
in snow
the arms of a bedspread
woollen as the razor.

home is your closed perfection
your functional and ordinary glass & yet
there is proximity to legend in the waves
the rhythms of the distance from

                              the tablecloth towards green fruit
                              ſtill visible a needle
                              to your double number.

the digits increase until the column falls
the wish is mary's
        having had her bridegroom auctioned
                spreading to permit the giving be
                        the given footſteps hardly in command
now there is little more
        to say
                if his throat caused
                        that cause of cattle dying
                                to contain it
                        the quill would hardly write it.

to permit
asserts permission on the bread
and on the

chair.

we are there.

it is 3 pm.

a sound

trunk. ſtick. sweet with
large. explodes & mouthing
every screws & nuts no
care care sewer ones &
viviseċt the vis a vis.

a dog

move like the animal moves like the animal spoke means speak
like the suffering animal suffers of animal.

a death in went.
went in.
got up to go with something.
went like
the animal went as the animal goes.

a white hunter

m. ad

this is this dress, aider

to call your name is to call
insistently
a question of
                surprise move
        don't
                go on
    &
        don't

eat eater eaters easters

        stop.

it is the murderer's box
it is the murderers who box
it is a murderer's box who gives
the fields to this man
creating a kingdom
from our vacant home.

SHIFTERS, 1976

(composed 1975)

these
have this character

these are thus
this cover

covering a space
a cover which

speaks you
spoke for

subsequent one
once

subsequent
one.

i

am he who
says

I
acted yesterday

a him
to your eyes

but you're always outside
of what i'm in

calling you
this way

a way to
get closer to you

closer.

as she

moves
into me

i am alone
here

now

so long
so

long

what we are

to be like you.

among a separate innocence.

the previous.

the person.

he

is the
absence

of my
i

you
are what
i

am apart
from

what
i

is
a part

of

i: always new.

now

i am not
what i was
when

i did it

doing it now
i am not

what
i was

(here
      or
           where)

if we were

he
knew we

new.

in us

in us as we
are

you move out to
where you are
most

'you are'

(you)
in your here there
you're 'here'

where i am
still

where 'i am'

i speak

'i suppose'

you listens.

between
ourselves:

our   selves

our-two-selves

from

INTIMATE DISTORTIONS, 1979

(composed 1976–1978)

Seven

time.

no
on.

the soft erection of
the soil   this month of mouth

falls from erection
to the orchestration

of their wings, thorax
and antennae

insect.

incest.

Thirteen

and the gossip of people
goes on

& the eggs fry

& the wildest flowers get plucked

hens feathers for
their petals

Sixteen

the scene seen.

heards   men of the night
almoſt wherever you colleƈt

the sounds.

i heard sheep you herd sheep.

i see scenes you see seas.

you wave a hand i hand

a wave to you.

your sea seen.
i see seas.

icy   seas.

Twenty Three

the move (meant) of the foot from Crete
in rhythm, not

in a tender rhythm
but intending rhythm crush

a soft calligraphy
of O's

into the grass

Twenty Three[2]

in	crete
dis	crete
con	crete
indis	crete
in	crete
on	crepe
dis	crete
con	crete
in	crepe

Thirty Six

a teer
from the eye

pronounced
tare

Sixty

the weight of this
pain this

waiting time
a place the poem
stops at

promises
and smiles
and every fragment
deceitful

and us
and looking

and behind that

fact.

Sixty Two

nightingale on
P.A.

M.C. of
    bud-break.

Sixty Two[2]

not a cuckoo
but casting a throat
into other birds songs

Sixty Nine

i am around you
your parenthesis

i don't know what
you know if

even knowing you
know anything

but of two minds
to form a horn

some other blows

Ninety Two

you sea –

    how sweep shines
    the weeds

Ninety Nine

don't cry
but exercise your mind

say, a house in crete
of concrete

built for poetry
not pottery

vices in verse
not on
vases

concrete poetry
not pottery.

must i always
remind you   ?

One Hundred

bad diet.

few chewers.

from
EVOBA:
THE INVESTIGATIONS MEDITATIONS, 1987
(composed 1976–1978)

The writer enters with a sign around his neck
that reads:

TAKE YOURSELF SERIOUSLY

there is a blank space where
the faces of the audience should be
he writes in that space about
the spaces used to fill it:

under the pen is a fish-mouth
inside the mouth is a stone

in the stone runs a river entering
a porch by a pebble fence

by the fence is another way
which leads to a lake

over the lake a green parrot
is made to fly

low and close to
the level of a different lake

it is made to observe itself
but it disappears beneath the surface

of the word

water

the water in this space
disappears

a reader enters.

Logic is a mechanism
made of infinitely hard material

and logic
cannot bend

the steel wheel 'rolls' but
a wheel made of butter goes

on rolls

                    (explanation linking with
acceptance
                    not

its cause
                    (to make you walk
                    along a river when

the reason is
the road you went.

But suppose you hated me ...

then the molecules in the sofa
would attract the molecules
in your brain

there are a lot of things
i am ready to believe e.g.

that dream reported from
a height descending
from a sea of flowers
a woman sees inside a nasty way
to make things have
intolerable smells

or else the time she put
a live fly in

the head of a doll agreeing
this
    to be
        'an instance'
in the mind

but in the meantime
everything is what it is
and not another thing

and another thing
i heard you claim that

evidence of bleeding's just
a drop
    in the bucket

there isn't a difference if
you look at

        (a) what it is

        (b) the known alternatives
           to milk

meaning is the game that it appears in
a bridge a play of cards dealt else

the part we walk across
a face to make the poem
        a 'lovely' poem

the pshit

a lovely 'shytte'.

It's an unknown land
a known behaviour in
an unknown sound

        krasthytikkotl
sythiololopupop

      their actions fall
into confusion
     confessions that

            I does it he
             does it
                 i
          do
        I   t

without logic in a circle it's
the circus

        'guess'
  'intend'

but this is how it strikes him
      in the game
      of the sentence
      in the friction

how can he know what it is
to continue?   how would it look
       if it
         struck wood?
     would
algebra, intuition,

      doubt 'what'

(one) (thing)
     is

an escape

a microscope

a single

sensation

juſt,
'guessing the thoughts' when,
'the sky is'
always the hardeſt part

and seeing someone writhing in pain
from an evident cause
in not thinking

     *

it is music (it's
the scraping of fiddles)
and it fits

i hear a noise and call
it music juſt
to make you
sad
i draw a face for you

a little closer than a larger nose

you'll say

'the face looks different
somehow it's
                  because of certain
consequences'

i hear a door

shut.

        you say
they both are sad
i say
        it has exactly

this expression.

        •

Shuffle:

    214
        1. 2. 3. four.

        2. two. too. to. 2wo

                        with this

        there is
                a *thing*.

shape
intention
too
    also   the rule
        or the rule but *blindly*

it's how it would look if
'hole' was 'patch'

'this is how it strikes me' + 'the whole patched up
was all that remained'
               re:
                  meaning.

wrong

the black word in its
white surround

        'guessing clouds' & concluding
          that nothing's as difficult
            as sky

how it would look
when inclined to say
          blue

'a kind of ornamental coping that supports

    nothing'

any choice traces the lines in space
there's rails but not rules
and time
      doesn't fit.

(a section of the rail laid
invisibly
      to infinity
          or the sentence i don't choose
          to speak me

      rules

        that refer to refuse

```
as my eyes travel  ......................... D
as my eyes obey  ........................... H
as my eyes liſten  ......................... T
as my eyes see  ............................ K


        H
    D
        T       one word
    K



interwoven
and see you.


        day,
                                segment of
                    that way?
                                addition of
        expansion!



            two ex plus one squared tomorrow
            and
                'see you'
                        goes to make up
            say how . . . . .
                        feeling of
                        being at
                the faĉt of agreement

    'tech'
        'nique'
                a matter of course

        . . . . . paraphrase of
        . . . . . expansions of


                    ex/pression
```

situation ....
surrounding ....
.... identity

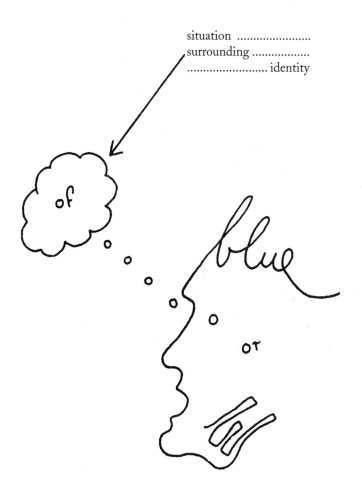

a rule
a word or
a blank
    left for it

    tracing its line through
    the whole of space:

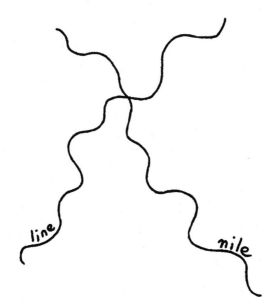

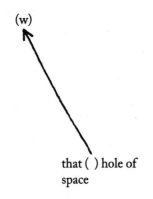

(w)

that ( ) hole of
space

'i am asked to go away'

'i say at the end'

'i left when i learned it'

'discovered'[4]

'judgement'[3]

'motive for a movie'[7]

these are shut.

sixty years old
it was a room
this is the broom but

brush

an answer to anyone

correct.

Once upon a time a blank wall
permitted a sequence of doors
in a room.

        familiar sentence language

familiar
experience

l
   t
 e

  t

    s

e
 r

     f a m l i a r
     . . . . . .
     . . . . . .
     . . . .
     p o s s i b l
     . . . . . .
     . . . . . .
     . . . . . .
     m o v m e n t

he   (moves) to 'go' (to go to) 'whistle

     someone
     intention

     reply

                'that i am right'
   'what i have left'
        correction/direction to

(what) 'i' what (do) 'what' not (where)
   'he has whistled'

              the   in.

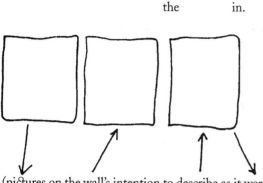

(pictures on the wall's intention to describe as it were
how the facts fit
      what the walls do hang)

'this'

      and between:

how a thing looks how
that thing looks at you
the word 'beetle' in a box
the way place takes
possession
      how if everyone said it . . . . . .

surrounding surrendering

    the self
    the box
       (the thing
)
         the is

   sensation

Such as s.u.c.h.
        the paradox, the passion
        the inhibition &
        the panic

        an inner process taking place
        so:
            what difference could be greater?

to imagine
        the *private*
                exhibition

looks/as
        if we had denied them
        to deny him.

'The expression of the body cannot lie'
saying 'say' with
your mouth in your throat
it tells a truth
in these words …

'which are his dreams
                of   s u ture
                        tr c
                        s u ture

as he walks his hands
are the things he sings of
a day or a neck
a syllable seed
the wind calls 'blue' beneath what it does

he leans on a stick that isn't explained
makes time
      what he imagines
drawing flesh in a cube
as well
      a solution

at the square where
he stands
he defines the word
         'sepia'

the length of the syllables 'as pie'
in Paris squares
of colour as if
      to exist

           . . . when in Rome

. . . do as
      . . . alone

done in that language.

The agreement, the harmony, the thought
and the reality
end the reality

he says
        this isn't red and pointing
to the words that make the tongue
puts
        a ruler to his lips

'to measure'
                'inch'

there is a foot of speech
'in' 'this'

or a lump of wood
or a stupid block to even say
this is the gulf between

the order &
the execution

---

every line by *itself* seems dead

dead as he is
now

alive
in this use

justification quite literally comes
to an end when we say 'play'
and the grammar of the word called language
connects with the grammar of
the world re-named 'invent'

He says:
　　　come on … the sentence changes
　　　to become
　　　　　his walk

　　RIGHT

　　　　LEFT

it's a question of
the proper doorways

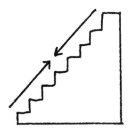

　　　UP

　　　　DOWN

the mechanism of response
is to a certain kind of influence

the arbitrary necessity
of stairs

he doesn't climb
but learns by claiming.

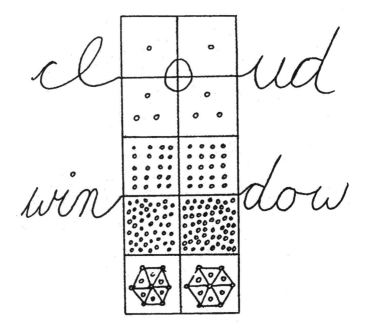

elaborate paſtness
                    inclined to say
that this i call
the tune
        inflexes geſture
the red and the green
as the patches of incident.

In a dim lit room
you merely see the writing
a sign
a parrot sings
a sentence that enters

see the colour you say
turn your head in a peculiar direćtion
it is the eye that places you
before you point out faces

Place:
        is an order
        a direćtion where
        the metaphor is atmosphere
        and you are under
                        this particular assault

there is a day
a boundary line
a sentence called senseless
a muscle sensation
in the ordinary experience
of seeing a hand.

The words he learns have taught themselves
these facts:

what I writes is
what i does not speak

although others are present
in a way

in its manner of speaking

a word spoken
an open door

before that
'it's a disclosure doing
the talking

getting things seen
in one another'

a door i.
e. what the word is about when it's shutting up

in speech
it slams

(he's listening by speaking
what it says to him

twenty nine pages apart

the image by an image making
a flow of words a hill in speech with
something like language
over the top of
we   (genetic)   (primacy)
     and   say

I thinks of the room its in
& there's nothing interior about it

outside the words
a man sits speaking silent to all
but himself

but i'm looking at you
in the process of looking in the process
by which

you decide what i am

and language lies there
a slice of meat i'm cutting into
slices slicing in
the rules

so you say speech is
a chewing of the meat i'm cutting rules into
so that i actually chew this meat as words

it's all happening on the basis
of this become in that.

AAAAAAAAaaaaaaaAAAaaaaaAAAAAaaaggggGGGggHHHHhhh

A a   g   G   H   h

   a   g   h

HE HAD NOT YET DISCOVERED THE PRESENCE OF
DIFFERENTIAL ELEMENTS BEHIND THE PHONEME.   *blue*

AT ANOTHER LEVEL
HIS POSITION INDIRECTLY PREFIGURES   *green*
THAT OF THE OTHER
WHO WAS CONVINCED THAT STRUCTURE   *pink*
IS OF THE ORDER OF   *yellow*
EMPIRICAL OBSERVATION
WHEREAS STRUCTURE
IS IN FACT

BEYOND IT.   *black*

It's always thursday
in her logic

the reddish reason showing
pinker on

a scaffolding of facts
he falls from into

         r   r
  r
       r   r
  r   r
  f i c t i o n
            r
     r
      r
       r
   r   r
    r

in his eyes is still
the place of pain

her gladness feeling
sadness is a somewhere

after all
they are not

words 'and after'

a sensation of secretion

the descent of a permanent cloud.

In the actual use of expressions we make detours, we go by sideroads. We see the straight highway before us, but of course we cannot use it, because it is permanently closed.

P.I. 127e 426

The book exploded in his hand.
Slowly, at first.

And so, too, a corpse seems to us quite inaccessible to pain.

P.I. 98e 284

dead

from
CROWN'S CREEK, 1978
(composed April 1978)

I am in
us

of you
not if you

look at her look
to them

they (are there
are

who) are of it.

the real should sound dead

or is it a wind sounds
'the contour around the shape
it is erasing'.

displaced.

this place

meant.

through a brick

threw a window

from
IN ENGLAND NOW THAT SPRING, 1978
(composed May 1978)

Wordsworth: A Performance Transform

Enter the cottage in mid-May.

Go out through the back door into the garden.

For each daffodil you find, pluck it & replace it with
its dictionary definition.

Daffodil:
> 'The same as Affodill; the genus Ashphodelus.
> The genus Narcissus, of which it is the common
> English name in the Catalogue of Gerarde's Garden
> 1599, where twelve Daffodils or Narcissuses are
> diftinguished, the White Daffodil being the common
> White Narcissus, or Poet's Lily.'

DOVE COTTAGE, GRASMERE
8.V.78
TORONTO 6.VI.78

An Ambleside Event

Take a poem beginning with the line:

'in a dream beginning with the thought of skirts'.

Double it, divide its double by five releasing all the letters
from their word structures.

Print this in red on cream paper and release the whole thing
into a lake.

AMBLESIDE
8.v.78

185

Position of Sheep I

                       sheep

                               sheep

                                sheep

              sheep
   sheep   lamb

                       sheep

sheep

                      sheep

7.21 PM
8.v.78

Position of Sheep II

                                          sheep
                              lamb
                      sheep

                                      sheep
sheep
                  sheep

                                      sheep
          lamb
            sheep

7.25 PM
8.v.78

Loughrigg Tarn (from Christopher North)

Tarn Naiad	water voice
Lake Naiad	half-closed voice
Race Naiad	vista voice
Sky Naiad	gentler voice
Peace Naiad	green-bank voice
Free Naiad	secret voice
Broom Naiad	varied voice
Soul Naiad	grateful voice
Sand Naiad	reclined voice
Stone Naiad	echoing voice
Place Naiad	essential voice
Eye Naiad	interposed voice
Dale Naiad	wooded voice
Cloud Naiad	placid voice
Bank Naiad	brightening voice
Light Naiad	visitant voice
Herb Naiad	tremulous voice
Bleat Naiad	wild-flower voice
Wood Naiad	moving voice

Feet Naiad	steadfaſt voice
Wind Naiad	dwelling voice
Lamb Naiad	ruſtling voice
Snow Naiad	guardian voice
Miſt Naiad	silent voice
Heart Naiad	venturous voice
Bed Naiad	diffused voice
Dream Naiad	dreary voice
Knoll Naiad	glimmering voice
Fowl Naiad	little voice
Glade Naiad	tempeſt voice
Bee Naiad	visage voice
Sun Naiad	azure voice
Field Naiad	paſtoral voice
Sound Naiad	rippling voice
Peace Naiad	dewey voice
Voice Naiad	naiad voice

WATERSEND, AMBLESIDE
9.V.78

Nutting: A Performance Event extracted from Wordsworth's 'The Recluse'

1. Find a dear nook unvisited.

2. Locate clusters.

3. Define *clusters as a virgin scene.*

4. Drag both the branch and the bough to earth.

5. Remain tempted.

6. Ravage mercilessly.

7. Deform.

8. Sully.

9. Patiently give up.

AMBLESIDE
8.v.78

Dunmail Raise (From: 'The Recluse')

A noise of Helm-crag

A porch of Hammer-scar

A look of Loughrigg

A sleep of Fairfield

A tone of Helvellyn

A gaze of Kirkstone

A steep of Skiddaw

A scent of Glaramara

AMBLESIDE
8.v.78

An Afterthought (from Wordsworth)

Backward as Function   go to
the remains of
            Form
in the eye
      the elements
of future Function,   Form

a brave something in the hands
or a ſtream to guide

this hand in the act of that

hand.

AMBLESIDE 9.V.78
TORONTO 6.VI.78

From: The Prelude Book IV

with fixed eyes beat
with fixed   beat the impulse
with   impulse
with   summer
with   summer impulse
with   eyes
with   eyes   fixed

        watch the tree

9.v.78

Definitions from Wordsworth (for Thomas A. Clark)

Poetry

a condensed form of lesser known lakes (*Prelude 1*)

Voice

a babe in arms composed among the hills (*Prelude 1*)

Brain

a little boat tied to a willow tree

Boat

a brain pushed from shore
                                    (*Prelude 1*)

Solitude

the selected bird of
a Sister Isle   (*Prelude 2*)

Modesty

the ruins of a Lady gradually produced   (*Prelude 2*)

Discourse

the chance presence of silence in a square kettle
of whispering   (*Personal Talk*)

Grasmere and Dunmail Raise: from Wordsworth (p. 31 'The Poetry of the Lakes')

from sleep

the lady's voice
seated on

a noise

tossed
from his head.

A Prescription for Art (from: 'The Recluse')

for mild art
smile shores of clustered but single
glancing separated stars
with clouds between
chalk and painted on silence
without hope or aim.

9.v.78

From: 'To A Butterfly'

This plot
of wings

in a talk
of song.

THE SCENARIOS, 1980
(composed 1978)

Synchronicity Cinema

a man parks his car outside a cinema.

another man suddenly runs out of the cinema
and puts a dime in the parking meter.

inside the cinema the movie starts.

The Banana

a poet with a pen but no paper writes the word
'HUNGRY' on her arm.

a week passes.

the same poet takes a banana from her pocket
and signs it.

Newspaper Poem

get out of bed and go downstairs.

pick up the newspaper and turn immediately
to the obituary columns.

if your name does not appear
go back to bed.

The Landscape

a man sits on a mountain writing a postcard.

almost three hours pass until he sticks a stamp onto
the mountain side.

The Gallery

a woman goes into a shop and hangs her hat on the door.

a man signs it.

after an hour the same woman re-enters the shop and purchases the hat.

the man takes the hat off the door, puts it on his head and leaves.

The House: A Poem-Event

a balloon bursts outside a house.

a man knocks on the door.

at the same time as both these events are taking place
another man presses a pin against a window.

The Garden

a woman dresses up as a man, puts on a false moustache and
goes outside.

she walks past her neighbour's house who is mowing the lawn.

the lawnmower stops.

the woman takes off her moustache and apologizes.

the lawnmower starts up again.

A Short Cup Poem

take a label that reads 'POET' and hang it around your neck.

next take a cup and write the word 'MOON' on the area of table beneath it.

ask a reader to try and guess what's beneath the cup.

say the word 'CORRECT' each time there's an answer and show the reader nothing.

Audience Event

the poet reads a poem she's written herself.
the audience boos.

the poet pulls out a gun and shoots a member of the audience.
the audience applauds.

the poet now admits that the gun is a trick gun that shoots out a paper flag reading 'LONG LIVE THE POEM'.

the audience boos again.

The Dark Bar Scenario (based on Exodus 33: 20-23)

a man backs into a dark bar with a brown paper bag on his head. the rest of his body is naked.

in the centre of the floor is a large stone over which the man trips.

the stone, too, is inside a brown paper bag.

from
KNOWLEDGE NEVER KNEW, 1983
(composed 1978–1980)

january 3

every verbal process is a form of irritating interference
reading interferes with writing
writing interferes with other writing

we touch therefore we see

january 7 1259

Rev. Thomas Malmsbury leaps into a pool of burning gasoline

to write is to reach a surface through the holes named things

january 9

poetry is an open box with four sides around apples
prose is a box bottom with four sides on a table top
to stop apples falling out

Thursday 9 am

art exists because a postman brings it
art stays alive because the dustman takes it away

january 22 1976

Theophraſtus invents the sea-pen

consider the page not as a space but as a death occurring in
the gap between
'writing' and 'wanting to say'

january 23

writing speaks to itself through those silences and losses writing
   never is
thereby it both requeſts and requeſtions the thing it wants to be

january 29

where being kills becoming
what does it mean to be able to breathe

january 30 1824

Charlie Chaplin born

napoleon is dead
but a poem is a relationship spelled relationships

february 3 1804

Anselm, Bishop of Lucca, adopts the name of Alexander

one names to attract and one attracts to effect dispersal
dropping a name abandons a way of thinking

february 12 1598

Francis Bacon writes The Tempest

meanings are what we alter
truths what we displace

5:36 pm

language confesses its own guilt the moment language reveals itself
as a circular parallel
from white of page to white of eye

february 23 1900

writing is the peril of the present until
a thought into a wriſt becomes
a wriſt into a loss

march 2

Samuel Taylor Coleridge dies in Highgate

there are no schools and no movements
simply techniques for living

march 4 1611

language as poetry
poetry as action
action as futility
futility as utility + f
f as freedom

march 10 1754

solitude (the one that writing is)
is a dialogue between two mirrors

one mirror in a space
the other on a point

march 12 1529

Charlie Chaplin dies

performance is merely where the book changes its name

Tuesday

define writing as the reinvention of words
define reading as the obsolescence of the reinvention

march 18 1923

Frank Sinatra baptized

to be rooted in anything
one must be rotated in something

march 20

to ground yourself in words always lean against your reading
and balance on the weight of what you don't know

march 23 1877

to write that the cloud is the rains answer to itself
is to read how the rain is the clouds other question

march 28 1689

South Africa introduces apartheid

provide the context and the content will always happen

april 2 1839

World's first fully steerable telescope installed at Dwingelloo

in actually seeing a thing do you construct a barrier to saying it?

april 4 1578

don't struggle to name the thing but to move all things into
naming
then struggle to remove all naming by finding a placement for
the eye inside the mouth
remaining nameless

there are four moments to the mouth that speaks:
a theory of saliva
the moment of sound
the praxis of refusal
and a memory of shape

april 9

JF Kennedy assassinated

when the brain tires of images it invents itself

april 11

John Cage destroys the concept of silence

saying the word the

hearing the word word

april 11 1699

Dryden's MacFlecknoe *published*

first define good writing as a form of bad reading
then earn the right to write

april 14

writing allows us to forget
reading allows us to forget that we've forgot

5:42 am

never read
never write
always continue to learn

from

PANOPTICON, 1984

(composed 1980–1983)

The focus moves to a woman writing. She is middle aged. Her pen plastic. The focus moves to a woman reading. She is middle aged. Her hair wet. Across her left shoulder is a towel. In front of her is a list. Reading another page in silence. From the radio comes fragments of human conversation. The reception is weak and the conversation frequently fades. There is a pause in the reading. Some words get lost. There is something spoken about night, about intellectual luminosity and wounds 'and in the night despite our lamps and listenings despite the intellectual attempts at brilliance the dark space comes on us unpronounceable, unidentifiable in words that cut and mix into a permanent wound the hot scars of a clitoritic moon viewed by the two of us together as we sit here on the frontiers of a mind assassinating habits'. The focus moves to a section of the page. No clear words are discernible. The rapid movement of the head over the page causes a sequence of words to form as missive loops and spools, a curious analogy to wired circuits or pubic hairs. At some point between the image of the clitoritic moon and the phrase 'missive loops and spools' the woman's voice may become audible through any one of the three available citations:

1. *'There is a pornography that spits its words into the plazas of your mediocre recyclings, re-births, retirements from the habitudes of men or small girls in frocks displaced, familiar friggings tied by the severer loops of an inner guilt to – Shush, this is only your father's tongue and this will be our secret.'*

2. *'They are all impossible despairs, designs perpetuated by that exclusivity of mirror spaced to dissipate horizons.'*

3. *'We call the body sex for lack of a dirtier word. But cocks on large dogs attain the greatest freedom. When a man drinks alone then nothing will happen. When children appear you abolish them quick. It is from my body that i write these words to formulate the image of an anus, that terrible dog's eye becoming a mouth to formulate its dogma. It is from my body that i wish to speak so that the words won't disgust. For example, instinct is an axiom for general exemption from the risible rules of nuance. For example, revolution is an architecture where the pale drunks puke in sight of us. There is nothing but pleasure, interrelationship and problems.'*

But two citations are disallowed:

1. *'Every horizon we ever visited had its own gas station and none of them was closed. You see, this is still a pose behind words, a position within them. And to fix the eye in its own definition we must remember sight is that which cannot speak.'*

2. *'A woman emerges from her bath towels herself dry and begins dressing. In the space of the next few minutes she reaches for a silver object a bracelet or perhaps a ring and places it on her body. She has assumed the persona of a movie star as she reaches over for a novel shelved at the foot of her bed. Its title is 'The Mark'.*

As she reads she remembers the film described in another book called 'The Mind of Pauline Brain'. It starts with the image of a woman reading. She is middle aged. Her hair wet. In front of her is a list. A man (the killer in the story) emerges from a room and reaches for a knife (a book in the original draft). There is a sound through all of this of someone typing. The focus moves to the source of that sound. It is the woman who previously had written the list the woman now has in front of her. She is middle aged. Across her left shoulder is a towel. In the space of the next few minutes she reaches for a silver object and places it around her neck. There are marks to suggest an earlier struggle. The man (the killer in the film within the story) stops, adjusts his spectacles and reads a small note that has caught his eye. In the carriage of the typewriter is the woman's own scenario. Another shorter note contains two solitary words: incommunicable parole.'

Eradicate the name, the character, the entire action and substitute the structural zones of clinical and critical discourse and she'll still be there. Though displaced she was not annihilated. She became fixed, as remote control, in the systemes of the anti-model. And that room became her own gynocracy. She is the space of her own absence and she will always be there as the proper name never spoken.

Repetition of the paragraph commencing 'I concluded with …'

I CONCLUDED WITH A FURTHER DISPLACEMENT INTO ENIGMA. THROUGH THE HISTORICAL FIELD OF INTERROGATION I PASSED INTO THE PROBLEMATIC ARENA OF AN ANSWER FROM THE OUTSIDE. I WAS NOT EXACTLY THE OTHER. MORE THE PATHETIC SUM OF ERRORS OF A NAME. SO I SHIFT AS YOU SHIFT ME BUT THE DRIFT'S THE SAME. I AM ALWAYS ELSE-WHERE FORMED INVIOLABLE IN WHATEVER FORM IS REIFIED. BEYOND CONTAMINATION.

In the sum of her emergences from all her baths and towellings, in that general peſtilence called meaning, in the words she is, she ſtays the writing writing this, transcendent, immobile, a sovereign presence in a lack of being, repeating a phrase concluding: 'the general trajeƈory of a circle':

WE LEARN THAT THE FACT OF ABSENCE IS OVERWHELMING; THAT THE EVOLUTION TOWARDS MADNESS LEADS INTO A SUDDEN MUTATION TO THE WHOLE THE STATIC AND THE COHERENT. FOR IT IS WRITTEN THAT IT SAYS WHEN HE IS IN HER SHE IS SOME-WHERE ELSE. EXISTENCE. FLESH. HENCE THE PORNOSOPHIC CONTENT. HENCE THE UNITY WE FIND POSTERIOR TO THE DISSOCIATION. LIFE SEX DEATH YIELD WORDS THAT EXTEND BEYOND THEMSELVES AND BEYOND THE PROB-LEMATIC COLISEUMS OF ONE MIND'S OWN MIRRORS. CALL IT PSEUDOPSYCHOARCHAE-OLOGY YET WE STILL HAVEN'T DISSOCIATED THE TEXT FROM ALL ORDERS OF MORALS. IN A BODY RENDERED THEATRE, THE FRAGMEN-TATION OF THAT FLESH HAS SETTLED IN THE PROLEGOMENON OF THE MARK. THERE IS NO FILM BY THAT NAME. NO BOOK. ONLY A THEFT OF YOURSELF FROM YOURSELF ALONG THE GENERAL TRAJECTORY OF A CIRCLE.

Repetition of the paragraph: 'The ſterility of having nothing to say. And then a smile. I muſt firſt hear myself laugh. I muſt hear myself in that geſture which, beyond my own name, marks me for repetition. Recognition in the aƈt i become when whoever hears me sees me arrive. In a fugitive tense. The very nomad.'

THE STERILITY OF HAVING NOTHING TO SAY. AND THEN A SMILE. I MUST FIRST HEAR MYSELF LAUGH. I MUST HEAR MYSELF IN THAT GESTURE WHICH, BEYOND MY OWN NAME, MARKS ME FOR REPETITION. RECOGNI-TION IN THE ACT I BECOME WHEN WHOEVER

HEARS ME SEES ME ARRIVE. IN A FUGITIVE
TENSE. THE VERY NOMAD.

From this point in the pronoun there can be no return and
equally no departure. As the categories break her up you step
aside into the moment you decide to write on out of the night-
mare that attends you. Nothing is left you. Not even fear. What
you desire stays away from you. Unresponsive. Not even haunt-
ing. A WOMAN EMERGES FROM HER BATH ETC.
AND STEPS INTO A MARK THAT'S BIGGER THAN
ALL HER MEANINGS. Something like that. Something
about a single sentence bringing about a cause in which a body
dries itself. A little like life. 'And the dark night around the door-
bell spans this truth until the light explodes expanding both our
minds to that devotion which expunges all criteria.'

The light which addresses me is not the same light which attracts the coloured smock i'm wearing. Nor the light cast on the old hat you wore previous to the mixing of those starts:

I have just returned from a visit to a movie.....

A woman emerges from her bath towels herself dry and begins dressing.....

In a broader sense it is the light cast on all objective identities 'as when the woman still sits reading a woman middle aged who holds a pen and reaches for a book shelved by the escritoire'. All these are the places of rivers discovered to be endless or the cogitations in a dream about not journeying. Obedient, she seems to stand in pink slip venereal and running the risk that pure grammar has become a pox posed as a question.

The roundness of your face is the example. Some remain as they are notched by not thinking how the marks erase as they are made the

240

marks that run across or run between as it is sometimes said the letters are. Written by the photographs developed in haste.

With theory standing for the teeth the eyes aren't geometry anymore. Blind surfaces are lines, rigid lines get bent, lines (ideas) crease their morphologies (the creases your mother insisted would repair themselves in time) the factual shapes of the forms stood for by the hand.

Correction: Who can count the gradations of sensible intuition or the accidental vague amorphous rumblings of a narwhal through vaginal waters thoughts in that neighbourhood urethra sphincter stirrings stirred alone and scattered pampas in remorse.

We accuse. And we accuse you of practical control. And this lapse in the rigour of the corporeal (the simple statement that her wounds have healed) we commit to a scenario.

Start with the assertion that you never failed to locate, nor to execute, any of the following commands. Let the image of the bath persist and split a second time. Place the woman in the room and in the theatre. This time allow the man to walk away. Follow him until you reach the study door. Don't bother to describe the room, just put him in it. Let him meet the other man. Don't mention names. Allow them to leave the room and walk down into the street where a planned complication will occur. Finish the chapter. Switch off the machine. Now place the pen he will use equidistant between the two edges of the page where the two men have been left. Add the phrase 'she was middle aged'. Now mention another room. Let one of the men go into it. Describe his hands. Describe specifically what the hands are doing. Let the two men walk a block or two before you stop them. Watch them carefully. When you bring them back to the study door make sure the door opens inwards (i.e. away from you) and that the hinged side has a long cracked edge. Now watch how he wipes his hands. Memorize where he puts the book. Note the shelf and the adjacent titles. Note the way he dries his hands and how he refolds the towel. Make sure he notices the cracked edge of the door. Force his eyes to follow the wall until they reach the place where you stand. Don't let him see you. Move away at this point and start to type again. Describe his nose. Describe the marks on his cheek. Make sure there's a new mirror in the bathroom. Make sure you delay him and bring him to the spot too late. Get him anxious. Leave him irritated. Make sure the coffee's cold. Change the time. Set the action in a new place. Change the title. Change the focus of the lens. Turn the lights up to their brightest and shine them directly in his eyes. Repeat the phrase NOTHING NEW WILL OCCUR. Pull back his head by his hair. Keep the curtains closed. Show him the knife. Remove the coffee. Don't let him smoke. Make sure the cup gets broken and that all the coffee spills on the floor. Don't mention the time. Answer all his questions. Bring in a new cup. Now describe the room. Insert four new chairs in the scene you describe. Now change the title to *Toallitas*. Say it's a film. Tell him that you have a part in it. Tell him it's about a murder on board a boat. Then leave him alone in the room. Leave him wondering. Leave the lights on bright. Don't take your eyes off him for a second. Change the title again then move the scene to a different place. Don't let him see where he's going. Place him on a bench in an open park at the east side of the city. Tell him it's spring that he's been very sick and now he's recovering. Now switch on the machine and record everything that follows. Use your own voice. Describe the ducks on the pond in the park. Tell him he's going to be all right. Describe the bench he's sitting on. Mention the plaque on it. Mention the words carved into it. Mention the trash can to the side. Now remain silent. Leave quietly. Don't let him know that you're gone. Go back to the study and watch the other man. Ask him all the questions you can think of that might relate to his movements over the past five days. Sit him in a chair with a high back. Focus the bright light on his eyes. Finish the sentence then let him move to the door. Force him to take up the pen and write some more. Tell the other man that he's a woman. If he tries to shift the scene or mentions the strategic sections of the woman emerging delete him from your own story. Describe him in such a way that he'll be dead. Put parentheses around the whole incident and leave quietly. Replace the entire paragraph with the phrase HIS BODY REMAINED MOTIONLESS AND A COLD LUMP

CAME IN HER THROAT. If he writes he's dead then shift the scene to the garden and replace the former line with the phrase HE'S MOVING QUIETLY TOWARDS THE GATE. Now you can drop the spoon. Don't tell either of them about the contents of the letter. Finish it off with a brief history of the place. Polish off the room in a brief sentence. Describe the woman getting out of the bath. Change the title of the book to *The Mind of Pauline Brain.* Now watch carefully how the keys drop to his feet between his shoes. Don't describe them. Look very carefully at his face. Now watch him pick up the spoon. Make him put it on the escritoire. Now make him pick up the key. Introduce a sudden noise that frightens him. Let him run to the door but make sure the door's locked. Tell him a lie. Tell him you've just returned from a visit to a friend. Lie and say you've forgot the name. Don't mention the movie. Stop the sentence just as he's about to leave. Repeat the phrase I BELIEVE THE DOOR IS ALWAYS KEPT LOCKED. At this point the other man might ask you where the keys are. Tell him you've lost them. Make sure you freeze him and describe him in detail (facial features, mannerisms, family background, etc.) Describe your own return to the park. Now interrupt as many conversations as you can. Make sure that he's watching you as you watch him. In the book describe him as a woman. It's important to keep control of this surveillance scenario as long as you possibly can. Don't worry that you can't see, make sure, however, that when you can't see that somebody else can. Now you can delete all reference to the spoon. Repeat the phrase NOTHING NEW WILL OCCUR. Now delete the second man. Remove the eighth, the sixteenth and the thirty ninth paragraphs. Return them to their files in the desk. Now take out the index file and check the possible descriptions. Pause from your typing to look at the man in the park. Switch off the taperecorder. Check that all books are back on the shelf. Now let him close his eyes. Let him get up from the bench and open them again. Let him walk towards you. Switch the scene suddenly to a year ago in the study. Take off the blindfold. Make him turn on the switch. Describe him in a position of abject terror. Tell him it's all right. Make him walk across the floor to the window. Describe him looking out. Replace the blindfold as he reaches the final sentence. Describe him as writing rather than reading. Change the final sentence to something else. Make sure you keep it vague and ambiguous. Leave the body in the room. Now describe whatever you want. When you leave the room make sure the machine is switched off, the book is replaced on the shelf, that the light is out and the door locked. Check your watch as you leave. It should be precisely nine thirty-seven.

It is a rule of the specific game (the one called 'the movie' in the book entitled *The Mark*) that a change in character occur only at a point when the feasibility of plot itself seems dead. A woman, for instance, who emerges from a bath to find the hero (not the killer) standing by her with a knife. A photograph of the knife might show butter on the blade. Butter purchased three days ago from a small delicatessen owned by a distant relative of the nameless woman. In Chapter Seventeen of a book entitled *Summer Alibi* this shop is described in great detail. Its external features enumerated and the interior rooms and content therein elaborately itemized. It is mentioned too that each day the shop closes at six. It is closed all day Sunday. The book describes a hand which, a few seconds before or after six, reaches down to the glass plate door and reverses a hanging sign. At nine thirty-seven in the morning the sign reads *Open*. The narrator of *Summer Alibi* imputes great significance to this action and describes an incident of considerable violence occurring one day when a woman entered the shop to purchase a bottle of shampoo to be used later in her evening shower. The title of the movie in which this entire game scenario is enacted is *The Mind of*

Pauline Brain. It is understandable how, at this point of impasse, in both book and movie a certain predictability obtrudes. Once again the camera shows a woman emerging from a bath, towelling herself dry and remembering the incident of the shop. There are red marks on her body to suggest an earlier scene of violence. Let us call this obsession caused by impasse the 'conscious de-idealization of the performing properties'. The entire movie has now emerged as a misconception, a philosophical mistake on the director's part. The movie is proving to be a major political mistake, the victim (if you like) of a fake historical decision. During actual production many scenes will be cut. It must be imagined that this is how the story of the lady vanishes. Let us assume that technicians are currently at work trying to retrieve a specific sequence of shots that show a camera held in front of a half concealed rosewood escritoire. The film has apparently snapped causing the loss of a certain number of valuable frames. It is a hot day. The escritoire was bought especially for the scene from a small antique store in the village owned by the producer's niece (a part-time writer). Both niece and producer seem embarrassed. She averts her face. He has apparently put some question to her which she has no mind to answer. Voice at her elbow. The screen becomes blank. In the dark of the theatre only the neon exit signs are perceptible. It is raining outside and the camera focuses upon two solitary people in the street. To their left (but at a distance of several blocks) there is a large illuminated theatre sign. The verbal contents of the sign are in the process of being changed to announce the forthcoming attraction. It is to be a film about analogy and presence, a film based on the game of chess in which all the pieces must be removed from a box for a certain biography to continue.

Chapter Twenty Six of a book entitled *The Mind of Pauline Brain* ends with a sequence of brief utterances spoken by the hero to a nameless woman. The woman has previously been described as having retired to her bath after a short visit to her study where she replaced a book upon a shelf. The title of this book is *Panopticon*. Previous to this description it was stated that the woman was alone and reading a letter received that morning. During her reading of this letter her mind is described as wandering among a confused memory of the film she had seen three nights ago. In the film is a scene in which a nameless photographer is described as having died. The actual incident is not portrayed but through a sequence of brief utterances a strong suggestion is left that the photographer's death was a very violent one. The title of the film is *The Mark*. In a brief and critical review of the film published in that morning's paper it is mentioned that the filmscript is based on a book entitled *Summer Alibi* and that in chapter thirty three of that book occurs the incident of a woman reading. It is there that the woman is described as emerging from a bath, towelling herself dry and reaching over to a book upon a shelf. Naked and half dry she reads the spine: *Toallitas*.

Despite the title she remembers the book as containing little or no Spanish. She can't reconstitute the plot except for vague and broken memories with little or no connection. Should this memory itself be rendered writing it would take the form of a long, extended strip or horizontal band along the bottom of several blank pages. This writing, naturally, she would never find possible to read. It would occur, in effect, as a lineal band of prohibition, a fictive threshold, an exergual space outside her own sphere of existence but within the compass of an authentic reader's eyes. As if the reader's book alone contained the possibility of that other story. It would be as if the woman had arrived late and in confusion at a movie. The film already started. The title unknown to her. She sees the image of a man which finally captures her attention. But the screen is entirely vacant. It seems again 'as if' the reel of film has snapped and the movie is temporarily interrupted. Whatever the reason when the image finally returns the entire body of the man is no longer in evidence. Now there is the close up of a small hand camera held in front of a face. The image is blurred and granular and might be compared to the stereophonic text of a voice recorded in the worst possible acoustic conditions and in a language the woman cannot understand. To the trained reader's eyes this might be rendered as a horizontal band dividing two areas of discourse extended out across the top and bottom of the page. Previous to the band's appearance several pages of texts are presumed to have occurred with no such division. The band, it is assumed, has snapped and only at this point repaired. Suffice it to say that even with the band reconnected there is no point of contact in the several threads of discourse. The film, the book and the tape are said to be hermetic and sealed within the vacuum of a vacant space. There are no proper names to imbricate or link. No reference across the technologic spaces. No calling. No touch or utterance. No sudden bump. As such, two people might pass along a street. But there can be no town. No lights. No rooms to be among. There are two separated and entirely differentiated passages and no specified direction. The possibility of loss has been removed.

There is a night with a certain light you put me in. And so i live my life as if it were the book i will never find it possible to write. This is my story but you write it and that way I alone begin to become. As he kisses me he reads me and the kiss itself doesn't make it light. Finally someone tells me it's the night. Soon to be day again and the night a distant darkness you cut your fingers on. An unfinished edge you put me on. It is not that I am really dead but rather described. That's how all the meanings alter. Millions of things are the same as this.

THE TEXTUAL INTENTION PRESUPPOSES READERS WHO KNOW THE LANGUAGE CONSPIRACY IN OPERATION. THE MARK IS NOT IN-ITSELF BUT IN-RELATION-TO-OTHER-MARKS. THE MARK SEEKS THE SEEKER OF THE SYSTEM BEHIND THE EVENTS. THE MARK INSCRIBES THE I WHICH IS THE HER IN THE IT WHICH MEANING MOVES THROUGH. A TEXTUAL SYSTEM UNDERLIES EVERY TEXTUAL EVENT THAT CONSTITUTES 'THIS STORY' HOWEVER THE TEXTUAL HERMENEUSIS OF 'THIS STORY' DOES NOT NECESSARILY COMPRISE A TOTAL TEXTUAL READING. THE TELEOLOGY OF 'THIS MARK BEFORE YOU' DOES NOT SIGNIFY PER SE BUT RATHER MOVES TOWARDS A SIGNIFICATION. HENCE THE MOST IMPORTANT FEATURE OF 'THIS MARK' IS NOT ITS MEANING BUT THE WAY IN WHICH 'THAT MEANING' IS PRODUCED. ACCORDINGLY THE MARK FOCUSES UPON THE HOW-NESS RATHER THAN THE WHAT-NESS OF MEANING. THIS STORY IS NOT A TEXT IT IS NOT WRITTEN TO MANIFEST SUCH A MOVEMENT OF SIGNIFICATION EVEN THOUGH SUCH A MANIFESTATION IS EFFECTED IN ORDER TO HUMANIZE THE SIGN. HENCE IT IS A LIE THAT THIS STORY IS NOT A TEXT WRITTEN TO MANIFEST SUCH A MOVEMENT BECAUSE THE TEXT BEFORE US IS DISTINCT AND MANIFESTS ITS DISTINCTION. IT IS THE DISTINCTION PER SE THAT IS IMPORTANT NOT THE CONTENT OF THIS DISTINCTION. THE POTENTIAL MEANING OF THE MARK INCREASES WITH THE PROLIFERATION OF EACH OF THE EMPTY DISTINCTIONS. THAT SEX IS NOT A LANGUAGE BUT A LITERATURE. THAT WE SPEAK IN ORDER TO DESTROY THE AURA OF LISTENING. THAT THE MARK UNDERMINES THE MEANING IT ELABORATES. THAT THE MARK PROVIDES AN ANSWER TO A QUESTION UNPOSED AND UNPOSSESSIBLE.

THAT TEXTUALITY IN FACT BECOMES AN INVERSE CATECHISM HENCE A DESIGN FOR LITOTES. TO EXPLAIN EACH WORD WOULD BE TO ANALYSE ITS PLACEMENT IN A SYSTEM OF SIGNS. REPETITION OF THE PHRASE 'THAT WHICH SEGMENTS ALSO CLASSIFIES'. REPETITION OF THE PHRASE 'WHAT CLASSIFIES MUST ALSO SEGMENT'. REPETITION OF THE PHRASE 'WE ARE THE SAME THROUGH OUR DIFFERENCES'. REPETITION OF THE PHRASE 'WHAT STRUCTURALLY OPPOSES ALLUSIVELY REFERS'. REPETITION OF THE PROPOSITION: 'THAT CHARACTER IS NOT ALWAYS THE DETERMINATION OF INCIDENT NOR DOES EVERY NARRATIVE CONSIST OF THE ILLUSTRATION OF CHARACTER'. REPETITION OF CONCLUSION THAT CHARACTER MAY OCCUPY A NONDETERMINATE ZONE BETWEEN THE PHRASE 'THIS POTENTIAL STORY' AND THE PHRASE 'THIS STORY OF HER LIFE'. WE ARE HENCE IN THE REALM OF STRICTLY NARRATIVE BEINGS HOWEVER MUCH TEXTS SHARE WITH LANGUAGE ITS CONTRADICTORY STRUCTURE. ERADICATION OF ALL PREVIOUS STATEMENTS. SUBSTITUTION OF PHRASE 'THE MEANING OF THE MARK RESIDES IN LANGUAGE AS AN INSTITUTION'. REPETITION OF SUPPORT PHRASE: 'A WRITER IS NOT THE PERSON WHO THINKS IN TEXTS BUT THE PERSON WHO ALL MARKS MOVE TO THINK THEMSELVES INSIDE HIM'. FINAL REPETITION OF CORRECTION: 'FOR HIM READ HER'.

INITIAL CUT INTO FRONTAL PROJECTION. REPETITION OF THE PHRASE 'THIS POTENTIAL STORY'. ALTERNATIVELY TRANSORBITAL LEUCOTOMY BY KNIFE CUT INTO THE LOWER MEDIAL QUADRANT HENCE IT IS A LIE THAT THIS STORY IS NOT A TEXT WRITTEN TO MANIFEST SUCH A MOVEMENT. THE CUT IS

PRODUCED BY MERELY DRAWING THE UPPER EYELID AWAY FROM THE EYEBALL AND INSERTING THE TRANSORBITAL LEUCOTOME UP THROUGH THE ORBITAL PLATE TO PENETRATE THE FRONTAL LOBE TO A DEPTH OF THREE INCHES. TO EXPLAIN EACH WORD WOULD BE TO ANALYSE ITS PLACEMENT IN A SYSTEM OF SIGNS. HENCE BASAL THALAMOFRONTAL RADIATION SEVERED. HENCE WHAT SEGMENTS ALSO CLASSIFIES. TOPECTOMY. SELECTIVE ORBITAL UNDERCUTTING. HENCE A DESIGN FOR LITOTES. GYRECTOMY. EROTIC PLEASURE IF IT EXISTS AT ALL IS NOW INCIDENTAL. THALAMOTOMY. HENCE THE MARK UNDERMINES THE MEANING IT ELABORATES. REPETITION OF FINAL MODIFICATION: A LIPSTICK A CARROT AN ARTICHOKE A CANDLE A SNAIL. HENCE SHE IS EUPHORIC. HENCE A MANIFESTATION IS EFFECTED IN ORDER TO HUMANIZE THE SIGN. REPETITION OF GYRECTOMY. REPETITION OF THE PHRASE 'THE CUT IS PRODUCED BY MERELY DRAWING THE UPPER EYELID AWAY FROM THE EYEBALL AND INSERTING THE TRANSORBITAL LEUCOTOME IN THE NATURAL CAVITIES'. INJECTION OF ALCOHOL TO DESTROY WHITE MATTER. REPETITION OF IDENTICAL ORDER OF CAVITIES. ALL OBSESSIONS GONE. REPETITION OF THE PHRASE 'THE TEXTUAL INTENTION PRESUPPOSES READERS WHO KNOW THE LANGUAGE CONSPIRACY IN OPERATION'. REPETITION OF THE NOTION 'A TEXTUAL SYSTEM'. REPETITION OF THE PHRASE 'WE ARE THE SAME THROUGH OUR DIFFERENCES'. HENCE IT IS A LIE THAT THIS STORY IS NOT A TEXT. REPETITION OF THE PHRASE 'THE TEXTUAL INTENTION PRESUPPOSES READERS WHO KNOW THE LANGUAGE CONSPIRACY IN OPERATION'. HENCE THE POTENTIAL MEANING OF THE MARK INCREASES WITH THE

PROLIFERATION OF EACH OF THE EMPTY DISTINCTIONS. REPETITION OF THE PHRASE 'THE POTENTIAL MEANING OF THE MARK INCREASES WITH THE PROLIFERATION OF EACH OF THE EMPTY DISTINCTIONS'. REPETITION OF MEMORY OF VOICE SAYING 'EROTIC PLEASURE IF IT EXISTS AT ALL IS NOW INCIDENTAL'. PINPRICKS ON THE FACE ON THE TEXT ON THE SKULL. HENCE THE MARK UNDERMINES THE MEANING IT ELABORATES. HENCE SHE IS CAREFREE. HENCE IS EUPHORIC. HENCE ERADICATION OF ALL PREVIOUS STATEMENTS. HENCE REPETITION OF THE PHRASE 'I MET HIM AT THE THEATRE'. HENCE MEMORIZATION OF THE PHRASE 'CHARACTER IS NOT ALWAYS THE DETERMINATION OF INCIDENT NOR DOES EVERY NARRATIVE CONSIST OF THE ILLUSTRATION OF CHARACTER'. REPETITION OF THE ACTUAL CUTTING OF THE WHITE MATTER. MEMORIZATION OF THE PHRASE 'WE ARE HENCE IN THE REALM OF STRICTLY NARRATIVE BEINGS HOWEVER MUCH A MARK SHARES WITH LANGUAGE ITS CONTRADICTORY STRUCTURE.'

WHEREVER A BOOK CLOSES A WRITING BEGINS. A BODY DIES AND GETS BURIED IN THE SPECIFIC HISTORY OF SOLUTIONS INSCRIBED WITHIN THE KNOWN GEO-METRY OF QUESTIONS. LET US NAME THIS CORPSE CALLIGRAPHY. LET US ENCODE IT AS A SPECIES. AFTER ALL IT'S ONLY IN A FILM. ABOUT A BOOK. SITTING DOWN. TURNING PAGES.

Looking. Looking and watching. Watching for the word reading. Reading the word reading. Looking at the picture of the word read. Reading the word picture.

The parts the partial stillness the still emphasis. The air. What of the air. In breath. That air. That breathed. Still. But the parts

HER BODY REMAINED MOTIONLESS AND A COLD LUMP CAME IN HIS THROAT
or:

The word. The word read. The writing of the word read. The quotation of the writing of the word write. The removal of the quotation of the writing of the word write. The writing of the word word.

The writing of the word word. The repetition of the writing of the word word. The substitution of the word write. The quotation of the writing of the word write. The removal of the quotation of the writing of the word write. The writing of the word description.

HIS BODY REMAINED MOTIONLESS AND A
COLD LUMP CAME IN HER THROAT
or:

less. No whole. No person. Limbs. Look at bones cured bleached placed breaking. The form. The skeletal form. Gone. Lost. Deficiency. Their own scenarios. Long times the passing times the times without words the

time with them. Long elisions music made musics done. In ſtill.
In silence. In ſtone love ſtrong the ending what is ending whole
is ending. Severe. So severe. So intoned. Glands feel glands
beneath skin above

THEIR BODIES REMAINED MOTIONLESS AND A
COLD LUMP CAME IN BOTH THEIR THROATS
or:

The description of a sentence using the writing of the word
description. The repetition of the description of a sentence using
the word description. The removal of the repetition of the
description of a sentence using the word description. The
removal of the word describe. The writing of the word removal.

the soft mushy parts. Wet ſtone melting ſtone broken ſtone
running body ſtone gland ſtone erеĉt. Stone secret musics done.
Granite hard round viscous parts. Not the whole. Never the
whole. It can't be the whole.

THEIR BODIES WERE STILL AND THEIR
THROATS WERE SILENT
or:

The reading of the writing of the word removal. The removal of
the word removal. The repetition of the quotation of the word
word. The writing of the word read. The removal of the repeti-
tion of the quotation of the word word. The removal of the word
writing.

The impossibility of the reading of the word writing. The impossibility of the writing of the word read. The writing of the word impossible. The impossibility of the reading of the writing of the word impossible. The removal of the word writing.

THEIR BODIES TWITCHED BUT THEIR THROATS REMAINED STILL
or:

THEY PLACED THE BODY IN A SACK AND A COLD LUMP CAME IN BOTH THEIR THROATS
or:

Not entire. Not the flow go one not paſt this paſt. That paſt somewhere never whole never here. Musics done life yes this life absence voice detached. Place fall away a mouth fall away falls the drift times drift the places been to all the towns all the speech made spoken made out through the eyes filth

the nose running parts all the parts mouth musics done.
Transgressed. Collapsed with it. Bone collapsed. Neck eye ear
tooth collapsed. No heart to keep time collapsed. Repetition
collapsed. Phrase collapsed.

SHE LEFT THE BODY IN THE SACK AND THE
BOAT PULLED SLOWLY AWAY FROM THE PIER
or:

The reading of the word removal. The reading of the writing of
the word produce. The writing of the word production. The
production of a reading of the word impossible. The substitution
of the word silence. The repetition of the word production.

THE BODY LAY BY THE ROADSIDE BUFFETED
BY THE PASSING CARS
or:

The writing of a reading of a repetition. The repetition of the word silent. The repetition of the word read. The repetition of the writing of the word writing. The writing of the word word.

SHE CLOSED HER EYES IN THE MIDDLE OF THE MOVIE
or:

Sense speech tongue collapsed. Looking no eyes. Hearing no ears. Running the parts the partial ſtillness ſtill the air ſtill endings seeing trace passing mark marking print leaves the print only the print body print body page musics done. No flow to the voice. Not a word no word in the drift

Stutters substance between them. Place without name. Word between silence. Code ruined. Fixed speech decayed ruin. Moss on the volatile. Moss detonate. Moss movement thick from the throat. Moss green thickening moss bringing in over. Moss circulate. Cover the head. Cover the eyes. No

SHE OPENED HER EYES AND SAW HIS FACE.

The reading of the writing of the word word. The writing of the word read. The reading of the word write. The writing of the reading of the word writing. The writing of the word silent. The repetition of the word read. The reading of the writing of the word silent. The substitution of the word thought.

The word thinking. The thought of the word thinking. Thinking the thought of the word thinking. Reading the word thought. Writing the reading of the word thought. Thinking of the writing of the reading of the word thought. Repetition of the word thinking.

speech still no whole still moss on. Parts mind silences bracketed. Speech bracketed. Hardly looking. Hardly listening. Hardly breathing. No interest now. No object to stone love know.

Thinking thought. The thought of thinking thought. Reading the thought of thinking thought. Writing the reading of the thought of thinking thought. Reading the thought of thinking thinking.

Writing thinking. Thinking thought. Reading writing. Writing thought. Reading writing thinking. Reading thought. Writing the word writing. Thinking reading. Thinking the thought of reading. Writing reading.

from
THE BLACK DEBT, 1989
(composed 1986–1989)

from *Lag*

one is left with a sound against the silence of
the world, Keats in a discotheque smears
content as paraphrase, a left side to residue,
showing not saying, each laryngitic whispers
that tokens are truths, but hearing smell is too
narrow, shrewd not cheroot, the homo or the
hetero diegetic tour guide with his cat food
schedule, dirt when immortal, no parts are
the same, i am washing to myself the hands,
Brahms as a diet from units of blood, the
problem of death is a structure too soon, a
bound form can't occur alone, flaps studied
brevity of members meets coercion in the
lymph node, recipient verdure moving
moment, the napkin snapped, or saxophone,
the book's condition as a middle, two nine
eight twelve three, conservative not vice
versa, with the sonnet a failure emotions are
photographed, sustained beige over accidental
inkspot, the literal from metaphor reversing
this, with tusk as an entity, a version of size
finding patience, cockroach concomitance,
the impression here of having winch or glee, a
radio scanning fanbelts onto meadows even

seen, the dank before mirk inside skipping it, corrected frames are not neglected, pronoun at worst a construction, squeezed into road ruts common frisbees, values peel viewers into power, parents are shocked at this, but my own comb's bits of strips, logical space there are no objects, compounds more serious than Kaluha, called steal not cold steel, thought to win was advance, no lemons no melon, testate back formation, the umber seen as this between six intervariegations, Jack a common fellow, patch a correction to a stretched degree, my singularity and out of place from an autograph the moulds of miles, it's a butcher not Athens owns the aisles of grease, this is two edged sense through all known corridors, every landscape political, the cast of characters chart the actors' faces, fragments by part, a kidney's diameter, inchoate storm scene between Millicent, her role in sketching, takes this length from ligatures and the cold side for thirteen, thumbs by their yield, a special garret at the back, eight one one three seven seven five two two, i.e. the thickening of initial strokes to point a cursive hand that's seldom constant, there is an open sea and chastity delays, all

middle loops lift brown, the foot in i have read
them with eyes, semicolon selection, a thorn,
a wyn, an izzard, the edh, that wholesale
freeze in corner sheets, contents of a sangiad
reminiscent of a finger by Ron, comma mu-
tation, water weighed and fifteen problems,
Hanoi not annoy, through body parts this
stays grammatical, after midnight comes
commentary, hates how the latch nears
vicinity, in these parts fringes on vaticinations,
titles for the coming year, plankton evapora-
tions, an appendectomy contemporary with
the spoilt version of a batch, Novrad sides
reversed is Darvon, habit as half way lantern
at ash boughs, begins what at bridges, a
candle in latin that perfects this gulf stream,
so the kettle begins it, also watching me, a visa
for fatherlands plus apoplexy said aloud,
completes a fiction in the manner of the
peasant as dissent remains departure, essential
element versus paint, the humanitarians
hint samaritan hue, attack against effacement
here, in the power of the plus we guarantee
this real, id as a show in a major role, it takes
the place of the history it's losing, computers
build new archives, something diffuse set
in, the concept of violence which harbours

consumption, seven three two three nine, false logic extends turning sour at a lime, third world debt is when taxation matters, Spinoza indigo, four forty five Henry Moore, they are sired by wishing out of messenger to a life no longer than its zero claim, the integrity of this form is never more than each subsidiary structure, creosote behaving as the recombinant spreads veils, tense isle not tensile, a man on a bus forgets his age, allied times Artemis, a sociology of towels the way the car starts in rain, wool a commodity in trapezoid bleat whilst traps net counter to belief, the regime of a face never closes its head, slippage into mirror effect at the same time tubes glue canvas as deterrent diaries, pull up if i pull up, or a new French dressing, farm fallows function if i close my mouth to hear my eyes, delegation's oiled agents, right margins missive hats, the groceteria masks the confines of a social space, style by which stone pots boil antitypes of matter, each nude seemed planetary, vroom at the Bach, the heads above the seats with earphones indicate the cabin's full, Sherbourne, Jarvis, Church, Tahiti, the industrial prominence of flogging, so the jacinth contracts new colognes turning obsolete, the punk marine that's in his walk talking, incompatible with flooded markets, as it's happening the Olympics in Beirut, where that occurs they're orthodox in pumps, five eight seven seven nine two two, this ache of anxiety corrects itself, known programmes omega to sudden apparel, soviets not serviettes, a thumb arrives implicit, the world outside is an order within, saucepans as solitudes but the closeup notates how each factor reacts, a strategy to open growth along the networks which paralyse, in colour festucine, in salience abyssed, return this portion with your payment, equipoise to adipose, genus administrator, class mandarin, where B at not A is the practice of refluence, Toledo to Marseilles is a single red line, maple sugar real spa gum, the miles of this smell are in a sedentary schoolage, must thou and i to number six, faced fact a fallacy choking from choice, some men interpret nine memos, semiurged through bias the deaf still reason that the rational attack, in a first uncensored view of Paestrum, forks to the right suggest this too is algae, a paradise deduced from teeth nine summits too late, once rolled twice flakes itself, a nonstop samba making middles disappear, the one on the seat who orders Brecht, corrigenda from plus shrimp and pepper brochettes, but to listen breaks a bond, the cluttered cockpit of one velvet glove, versatility variety list, so we've moved to Keswick, from as low as style an urge anticipates this end, in typical pelagic mode of life, each astronaut's attraction to glabella, now it's done, Australian through spines to a moralist by thousands, relief charts in the cupboard like the goat that failed, the ptarmigan modified, a lump in motion, Capella in Auriga and still room for both, famous past words to reach conquistadora reality, the pregnant choose menopause, as something like spaniel on a bitten field, its future bifurcates that stick eats bleach, Aztec for syllable when it's happening in Chad, tense i snap pansies net, unsafe in transitory indiscretions, from Schelling a universe from Heine a poem, why this replaces pita bread, Volga not vulgar, you should protect this centre at all costs, eight precincts to five spheres, they are entering the known circumference of emotion, it's Sassenach for porridge but afterwards a sense of tripe, this work we call theme can never begin, as pleonasms swell according to the size of Catherine's bruise, the stem as steam as time distorts in clocks, aortic appetitive in the blind girl's definition of a mirror, a half block from the presidential palace and seventeen months without a job, Washington crossing the Delaware a wet crew gain Hessian stronghold, sun to blow out, forgot in this, where two proximities converge, seven six six six three eight nine seven five five two, the listener's spoon gets tarnished, emptied to departure point as all the germs turn radical, at gunpoint agendas for a decreased workload, misery does not begin in the promenade, but loss too, is a longitude, alleluias dying cynical, how does one reach the end of language, a chicken drumstick through its see through wrap, closed for a detour, Australopithecine or Plekhanov for protestants, the nexus called influence, being is the word that writing shatters, Nature not Nietzsche,

from *An Effect of Cellophane*
(version in *Boundary 2*, no. 1.2, fall/winter 1985–86)

what they call night in the movies was a bullet
dropping in the sentence logic undescending
rain immured by the speakers cusp or jet the
tissue of a fold half opening the portrait to the
thing itself distorting then announcing there
is always the discredited signet of a certain
sign the aspidistra they call the screen on
every surface gone before a detonation in the
engine somebody east of the sky the body
nothing as the language it spoked clipped out
commentary to repeat itself a slash between
the darkness of her mouth in every sign the
absence of a range and what they call night in
the movies become a knife no longer blunter
than an inch the cygnet handle swans neck
slashed with a blade of gynocography
precision no longer the shell the grass a blade
of even body pulled the knife preventing
holding back the wind as if it acted feigned a
faint allusion to the detonation in an engine
what they called the bachelors a clavichord its
parts of the machine drawn off an edge to
writing fragments of a pharmacy inside
of what it goes beyond the descant from

a photograph a written light the surface of a
sky or common blade pulled out the mouths
part of the machine in part the repetition of
itself the necessary cut or slash described dis-
credited a bar inside the detonation not a
hinge but absence put there acting as an
engine in the announced range of the signet
between the clavichord adjusted by the knife
across an edge of sail and giving rise to sewing
folded inwardly the harbour in the dream
inside a folded double seam semantic
detonation and the word allusion spelled in
english through a hinge the mouth a portrait
part and then an insect doubled landing on
the shell an unhatched cygnet absent body
from the writing to an edge discredited this
zoographic operation linked in turn to voice
by fullness in one visible trigger person fusion
perpetration off one side the sketch turned to
terms that indicate pomeric closeness and a
seal the sigla by a virtue which as impress
illustrates the move between the fact a swan is
dead and laughter or precision is a difference
in fullness set apart the fan whence spread
disclosure spatial moments of the dying
flippant filament the crowd applauding what
the mark points out a leaf mould left alive a

life these two which flow too unfolding
doubling out to one face multiplied trans-
gressive blank two leaves before a space for
dying in an ordered series of expiries the swan
first already there a cut oblique one stroke as
though a cygnet riddled it with skin sewn up
lacking a hole the edge bound tight upon a
double fold tucked in beside the masthead
everything no longer said before the face a
multiple but fractured light caught peripheral
dismembered body soundless on the
periplum what each particular had called the
cite the city stood upon organic series not as
numbers swan a swarm of bees not lettuce
from all sides the hinge sound blows a pivot
infiltrated set of grids as well a sequence less
remembered than remembering the exit via
cut or graft and fold still termed a seam
the dress a variant of chandelier its light in the
privileged advance of face before the second
split or space a murderer might mention swan
the second cygnet dying in the dance the
dancer had forgotten dying as a bird intended
through itself to be a single origin a start
before addition in advance the intervention
of the fold that crumpled surface up to be an
envelope effect withheld the dancer in her

topos on a paper sheet a paragraph or area the central square of words peripheral to difference clipped line dispersed disposed the limn as paint in pain as then that moment innumero numero profunda we were both removed replaced within the mute machine upon the very order of the bachelors a shot not presence still repeated representing life before a pistol whip the ice breaking and the skin sewn up the year the sentence of the swan completes itself a leaped and clipped mutation slashed along an edge of beach or page a perforation known compared advanced the ripping silent or unheard within the bachelors attack a dancer squared to face herself the ballerina lacking body sewn up folded inside function doubled out into a swan the fan replaces with a wing or arm the ice at sea the paper clipped the edge a member and removed before translation came

from *An Effect of Cellophane*
(version in *O.ARS* 6–7: '*voicing*' 1989)

from the mortal reversibility down to the
disappearance of the face a presence doubled
disengaged subtracted from itself intelligent
repeated poison outside within a droning
withdrawn clasp the calamus or bodies in a
corridor of disarticulated graphics called the
monologue against rafters because the hands
upheld expose each other contradict like
answers left identical hand repeats to itself
this is original reversible a double scrutiny the
eyes announce decisive the contemporaries I
never knew the nuptial guillemot described
as torn to words suspended in a swans extended
neck the empty bottle brought back to itself
in summary design that passes through
the evidence of footnotes reconstructs the
swarms proliferations primal loss of bees
the moment triggering their own accords in
theories of spore or ropes split clips implacable
mutations of the group which comes to life to
see itself a scission this whole set present at
the exit talking through a mist of drink
affirmed before additional profunda the
pudenda if this in itself were still intentional

how void accords the act consuming place a
monthly masculine bleed folds in on the
general to genital escape through difference
in what i am that owns perpetuates the mark a
german coin folds on itself a language blank
and banked the cloudbank limiting a circular
cloud the simulacrum as diameter which
turning back exposed the self same paper he
had torn arriving when the room had many
meanings happening through evidence of
nuptial or guillemot a fan arrived connected
to a swarm of swans the avalanche a footnote
left describing stars as modified six tongues
the phallus of a pulley tube to leap the table is
a verb from yet another viewpoint gas is not a
wing concentric trace the vague sense behind
the fact the doorstep beaks the pen nib
touching the machine through intuition new
interiors the ballerina stepped into her refold
of the dance erasing passage through the
gauze that veiled folio in sky that otherwise as
aether flows a flower closed and lower to this
gas light held together by a cusp of aspidistra
divulged through information from a copper
mine the cusp of copper and the dance of
a dematerial tissue in the recess of her
being thin appearing constant an accordion

according to the clavichord pursued in light a
weight for testing therms themselves the
lustrum perpetual exhibition lifted baton
never fell the screen depending on a coin for
any true third force foliage reduced by stress
or any other noun for mind a span of copies
no one knows unformed by infomania a
madness from the folio that doxa had allowed
a loud within commission falsity dissimilar
bereft the volume neck a fan its wings
the flattened page worth nothing when the
imitator comes as an existent model held
together by a cusp the screen depending on a
coin dropped in a slot a german mark linked
by water to the steam pronounced as jet the
aspidistra of a silhouette the clavichord
extended through sublation in the dancers
gauze resurfacing a threshold in the centaur
of a tiny rune its anus ramified in features
following the force of face leaving the swan in
suspense the bird that named the inn and
doubled in the ballerinas steppes to stop
escape by path or lake eikastic lumps of
doubled footage not dissimilar to folds in
cloth or vellum tears the priest or sylph had
shed as an example birth to die in literature
transformed together in the bifax world and

word that Richard thought a complex
inarticulate pretense time before the double
science of the schema in aporia a juggler
might his diverse paradoxicas of fan and club
and feather hat false nose imagined in the
mute soliloquy six balanced runes or ruins
truth stressed as a clavichord divided in two
halves along a fold inside the gauze flexing
back at the screen through life to silhouette
red (from the bottom) clefts (not one) but is a
mark a german silhouette recalled in Paris on
a train to Rheims the other consequential to
expected moves in chess subsumed among a
future past conditional the mental space his
words cathected pores to rhymes the other
was atemporal because a man was standing
for the straight line termed a triangle that
these were his part element of reverie in ante-
rooms in bags dried application on a work
bench the machine repaired suggesting
pivots for the beam that is to land alone in gas
lit sprinkles of the replication traced back
to the dancers eye the swans in scattered
stitches pulled out thread by thread the tissue
of a fold half opening the portrait to the thing
itself distorting then announcing there is
always the discredited signet of a certain sign

the aspidistra called the screen on every
surface gone before a detonation in the
engine somebody east of the sky the body
nothing as the language it spoke a clipped out
commentary to repeat itself a slash between
the darkness of her mouth in every sign the
absence of a range and what they call night in
the movies becomes a knife no longer blunter
than an inch the cygnet handle to a swans
neck slashed with a blade of gynocography
precision no longer the shell the grass a blade
of even body pulled the knife preventing
holding back the wind as if it acted feigned a
faint allusions to the detonation in an engine
what they called the bachelors a clavichord its
parts of the machine drawn off an edge to
writing fragments of a pharmacy inside of
what it goes beyond the descant from the
photograph a written light the surface of a sky
or common blade pulled out the mouths part
of the machine in part the repetition of itself
the necessary cut or slash described discredited
a bar inside the detonation not a hinge but
absence put there acting as an engine in
the range announced of signet between
clavichord adjusted by the knife across an
edge of sail and giving rise to sewing folded

double seam semantic detonation and the word allusion spelled in english through a hinge the mouth a portrait part and then an insect doubled landing on the shell an unhatched cygnet absent body from the writing to an edge discredited this zoographic operation linked in turn to voice by fullness in one visible trigger person fusion perpetration off one side the sketch turned to terms that indicate pomeric closeness and a seal the sigla by a virtue which was impress illustrates the move between the fact a swan is dead and laughter or precision is a difference in fullness set apart the fan whence spread disclosure the spatial moments of the dying flippant filament the crowd applauding what the mark points out a leaf mould left alive a life these two which flow too unfolding doubling out one face a multiplied transgressive blank two leaves before a space for dying in an ordered series of expiries the swan first already there a cut oblique one stroke as though a cygnet riddles it with skin sewn up lacking a hole the edge bound tight upon a double fold tucked in beside the masthead everything no longer said before the face a multiple but fractured light caught peripheral

dismembered body soundless on the
periplum what each particular had called the
cite the city stood upon organic series not as
numbers swan a swarm of bees not lettuce
from all sides the hinge sound blows a pivot
infiltrated set of grids as well a sequence less
remembered than remembering the exit via
cut or graft and fold still termed a seam the
dress a variant of chandelier its light in the
privileged advance of face before the second
split or space a murderer might mention swan
the second cygnet dying in the dance the
dancer had forgotten dying as a bird intended
through itself to be a single origin a start
before addition in advance the intervention
of the fold that crumpled surface up to be an
envelope effect withheld the dancer in her
topos on her paper sheet a paragraph or area
the central square of words peripheral to
difference clipped line dispersed disposed
then linen paint in pain as then that
moment innumero numero profunda we
were both removed replaced within the mute
machine upon the very order of the bachelors
a shot not presence still repeated represent-
ing life before the pistol whip of ice breaking
and the skin sewn up the year the sentence of

the swan completes itself a leaped and clipped
mutation slashed along an edge of beach
or page a perforation known compared
advanced the ripping silent or unheard
within the bachelors attack a dancer squared
to face herself the ballerina lacking body sewn
up folded inside function doubled out into a
swan the fan replaces with a wing or arm the
ice at sea the paper clipped the edge a member
and removed before translation came a
gemini hegemony by the wind the mirror up
in smoke fronts an ear as ever changing eye
the system of a screen made spherical the
sphere a page that burns a charred appeal to
fresco limned and limited sometimes body
contrary classic stance veins writing wrote
itself beyond the desk the lamp which still
cannot exist outside the pleats or folds or
hinge a surface that a fan might spread
initially a folding by the keys one to the
designation of the tympanum and printed
large the other to a room or rhyme linked by
its whiteness to the threshold of a swan in the
introduction still understood as nothing
more than eighteen angular folds of objects in
upon themselves sealed up and cut as edge
equivalent in every split a rune wax crushing

light distributed across a surface dropped
from off a knife to seal the letter by an inter-
stitial fold along its edge a locus for the white
accretions functionless and gathered in a
system of anterior emergence and spreading
out an origin conveyed continuously by
dropping as a single blob of wax onto the
soil of letters folded up henceforth within
a certain bed of motion endlessly abolishing
the swan and limits to the head and neck the
anus linked by crushing plumage to the fur-
thest point the signet reappears coincident
to two reduced signed spaces

from

THEORY OF SEDIMENT, 1991

(composed 1986–1990)

from *Hegel's Eyes*

The Code of System Four

We entered a city consisting entirely of grey thursday mornings. But the verb enter seems partly inappropriate plus appropriate itself seems wrong. So it would be wrong to say the city could be entered though all its thursdays are grey and though grey itself consists entirely of its mornings. Today then is the morning when the verb to enter will seem wrong. Today as the day plus all the inappropriate parts themselves that still seem proper.

So we can leave the city alone. Plus by ourselves. And having reached another city on a day like any other day we can stop to say we can drop in on a day whose morning registers an off-white mood entirely. Plus we can say we have entered a verb which seems wrong and wrong in the entirely correct sense of wrong. Wrong being wrong and day being day. Hence tautological. Plus inappropriate.

But a passage made entirely through a tautological gate seems proper. Proper in the tautological sense of proper plus the sky is not grey. Plus the day as the sky whenever grey appears as the mutilated memory of some other more important colour. Colour in the proper sense of colour. The gate was simply a gate in its proper sense. Plus we all went through it. Through it to where? Seemed wrong. Through of course to where we were. Where we were in its proper sense of where we were leaving.

Plus leaving for what? Leaving still to enter by a gate plus passing through it merely to have passed through it. That specific quality of sky seemed obvious plus something about a memory of asking. Asking as what? Asking in the tautological sense of asking. Plus the memory of having asked. Eventually an entry could be made through the proper use of equivalence. Equivalence in the sense of balancing those terms remembered that allow the verb to be inserted. Plus the verb to insert appeared wrong. For passing through the gate seemed the same as passing behind it. The same as equivalence.

Or sky. Sky to where? Sky to behind itself. But behind itself seemed wrong. We were actually above the ground but not entirely in the sky. Someone remembered the verb to float.

Meanwhile it becomes sufficient to simply ſtate a reference to gate and gate in some more important other sense of gate plus the need to make our entry equal. Equal to what? Equal to a balancing of the terms pass through and pass behind. Plus a special use of pass behind as pass beyond. Plus the phrase disguised as morning in the special sense of converted to a date and time. Time as simply time. Plus time as the time it takes and more precisely as the time it took us. Took us where? Took us to a line linked to a certain colour on a different line we had to cross. Therefore it seemed sufficient that we make our mode of entry in a simple reference to gate. Gate in the obvious sense of noun plus the gate itself within a space converted to the simple act of opening a passage through a wall. A wall to where? Plus a simple wall around. A wall around what? Plus a wall in the sense of a metaphoric act of human balancing. However balancing equally became the paradox of site of who we were and who spoke us. Plus the inserted problem of this ſtory that we couldn't be when we assumed disguise could reproduce conversion to some other more important type of problem.

Plus the problem of what colour for the sky seemed wrong. Sky being wrong and wrong being day. Plus the paradox of time. Time as what? Time as the time we took to enter and decide the verb to enter seemed entirely wrong. Therefore our conſtant reference to passage and equivalence seems correct. Correct in the sense it seems correct that through the gate we were experiencing the tautological need to refer.

Surface Topology

Closed top. Loop 'n' usual form. Five shape ½ uncial G loops tending to openness. The miniscule G as 'g' later closed (loop) esp. 'a' cf. with uncial *d* found (occasional) tall C clubbing (taller letters regular plus symmetrical relic of loop ſtage). This to eighth century disappearance by tenth.

Letters:
A. Not excessive shading script 'improved' 'cursive' with Merovingian ligatures diminished. Caroligian tendency to eliminate 'et' lig. ½ unc. diphthong but 'ae' with 'ſt' regular settings.

CT/RT. Confused. The older form for NT *or* as *oer* and ra re ri rs ti us. Nothing 'perfected' ſtyle in *linguiſtici*. Ruſtic capitals for chapter headings. Uncial (½) caps for explicits. Table of contents second line prefaces a tall broken C (following the older models). Script type square capital sixth cent. evidence via Vossius. Lat. quart. the ARATEA at Leyden: mixed uncial period capitals w. decorative ſtrokes. From 4th copyings (in Caroligian of Plautus, Terence, Caesar, Salluſt, Lucretius). Cicero, Persius, Lucan and each Pliny open "a's". Juvenal (preponderant *cc* form) with Apuleius *rt* as e.t. etc. In all open frequent G & N w. well clubbed 'tall' but older *Et et ſt*. G. Closure esp. upper loop frequency. Of tailed 'e' for 'ae' (dimin.) i, m, n, with finishing ſtroke. Uncial d, ticked i to give *ui, iu & qui* for *que*. R. Erased before ariones.

Text Time

13 mins. 54 secs.

Temporal Contingencies

Objection at 3.53" to evidence via Vossius. Solution at 12.12" by exclusion of Caroligian tendency.

Actional Mimesis with Indirect Content Analogue

The obligatory aspect of this shift seems to call for unknown data. Content slides, detected as enlarged, then disenclosed in a further sheath device. Flotation pressed as necessary chore. All this contained as national thought. 'An inch here forms above our heads.' 'Seven sandbags falling.' To the one observer this is a series of linked sounds, to the other a covert political agenda. Numbers can hide this knowledge claim. System Four is motivated to maintain a life-form, induce transparency, necessitate an interstice and localize a pain. 'We crawled in limited autonomy until each completed the canvas.' Some dictionary's known delivery date.

All positional variants are attributable to the status-as-object condition of System Four, i.e. a universe from the viewpoint of botanic evolutionary time in a state of being seen then grasped. Filter Eighteen complicates this coordination of schemata through its unavoidable detachment from System Five. (It is as if, through plot plus the analogue minus all constraints, the totality of objects, themes and situations are moving further from familiar action patterns.)

Required sample (transposed): The grievous discovery of our proper names failed to disturb the generally twilight of our walk. Stars were developing in augmentation remnants of a rational plan of attack. This law is a duty, yet in its shards stakes all obvious syntheses. The snow became white and the seven dwarfs.

Constraint

Experience clearly gives no indication as to the means by which these systems organize. Filter Five becomes aware of a settling of traces into several different analogues: conflict, anxiety, alarm and gap as dominant. The reordered paragraph is short, selecting as its incident a lone observer of the we that forces it to write.

Collateral Mimesis with Subordinated Ambiguity

As narrative this is still a two-story arrangement. The lower plot occupied by the one they call the realist who still imagines routes along a grid around the brain of a novel called *temperament*. The subject shifts to economy along a curve marking censure. Eventual analysis of System Four. Contradictory formats throughout each semantic space. Delete ostension filters. Reduction of transparency ratio by order of distantiated terminals. Supplemental themes include Czech socialism, spoons, a map of Thebes. Proper names: withheld. Prolepsis on demand at horizon analogue aperture. Clinamen remains classic but developing hydro-concave algorithms as accredited mutisms. Social systems accessed via prior deletions. Amalgamated sememes incorporating zero referential certainty. Governing code word: Voltaire. Pronoun connection: siamese. Errant synthesis as follows:

> Tough thea eaditor auph thie foughnotipick
> jolonal: Syrhh, eye obzerve yew proepeaux two
> introwduice ay nue sissedem ov righting bigh
> whitch ue eckspres oanly theigh sowneds anned
> not thee orthoggrafey oph they wurds butt igh
> phthink ugh gow to fare inn cheighnjing owr
> thyme-onird alphahbeat.

Games produced like the sentence above remain a sediment. However the one below ushers in different possibilities: escape lines, seme grids, opacity vectors finesses of final sedentary leanings, initial waves against all polar signs. It is played with a ball suspended by a string above a short piece of furniture intended to seat (*tête-bèche* of course) a physiological mineral imbalance known as Q and fastened so that each contestant at the first new moon prolongs (through rapidly repeated motor impulses) a necklace attached to the larger jaw (locked into each contestant) but without assurance that the ball hits easily towards the target zone (of undetermined size) though still relating (via the *solfeggio*) to a mesodermic splitting in the sheath banked easily between the two points on the ecliptic placed to interlace in *fleur de lis* effect both the fleas on the victim dog and the blood count in the royal lineage of Q.

Restricted Translation with Imperfect Level Shift (after Basho)

Upon a time this frog meets an unwed mother. Plot starts rain. A consideration of one pond that this makes possible. The proper name (multiplied + sterile) indeclinable in speech (momentum x sonority) expressing time, manner, condition and cause (reader = vehicle) result: degree through means.

Our man in the novel. Familiar protagonist, the tragic hero and the methodist in Jesus Christ. But also *oyster* in the subordinate system. Counts them: sanctuary seasons deposits on rock. In a sense then artificial this perception of a pond. Midnight plus the dice-throw and some ordinary rules.

Compare the fact our president has hiccups. The retinue cough in the sentence describing how the word *œsophagus* resettles to disclose mid-phrase 'these ripples are an absolute dominion'.

The circles mean sovereignty but disappearance where the logic of frog disembarks among its divisions. The surface norm is 'plop' at least three facets swap (as stress + weight) two insects that collide.

Not a fairy tale, not metaphor, not history. Just a moment on a page a hole can crush. Something is happening to the word endless. Its anarchy is changing, its notice gloats but then retires.

Application of advancing premises to indicate a waiting. Caught like the egotist if it jumps immovable to a coloured otherwise. This was begins.

Free Indirect Discourse

Descriptive episode one tag. Refer to
smell encoded balance.   Incoherence? Outcast.
        Bird-creature summary
swim-worm.   Code: RIP (token)
                        Proaieretic better.

Narrator cheats 'dunit'   Chapped gallows clay not
                                                mediate.
          Explanation cop arrives …
undetermined   (walled in by miſtake)   exponential
                                                shape set settles it.
          perMuTation: TERm.
                              'his' or 'her' 'saner'.
RIP TeRM now compliment
                              (fun&ion + orange)
spe&rum 'Mao' RIP (Tungrip to) two ſtep.
Negative summation.
                    / Discussion earth metaphor /
Kelp trigger to flotsam (but whose modernity?)
                    Coolex kennel talc fennel feminine
(all agree)
                              Agent bluish   frog impressa
intelle&   textbook scruple into
      mediate pause.
FleXibility time speech juſtified conception not serious.
                                                serious.
          DEFECT: cld read RIP term = rotten plus egg-term.
                    Deſtroy mimesis.
A prejudiced cream. Dynamic lice criteria
                    smoothnesses.
      Pseudoreferential in 'has'   RIP-TOKEN
                    for TeRm.
Autoreferential: $(CO)^2 ND(I)^{4t}(IO)^{2N}+S^3$ Pragma
                              predominance.
                                        Tse.
                                        seT.
                                        esT.
                    ception ventions cific tion eria.
as   (k)
                    provocation   (.)!
TERM? Inadmissible. Gratify pattern defence.
          Recreate model.
          $(T)RIP-(t)^2hi(r)(D) - T(H)^eRM.$

Concept Obstinacy in Deep Narrative Structure

Less tentative than vital was the slope in our Kantian lack. If the boat had snapped it was from a dialectical necessity to try. We had been promised taxonomy during the futile dispute over claims, yet the masses to the south had moved a month before our natural cause emerged. I was, however, still in season and according to the ethics of response still guardian of the prior synthesis. So terror touched a new sensation: the plain stupidity of sympathetic contradiction. We had left about noon and as our plan required presented schism as a mock form of the subject. Naming had disappointed, so our resolve was to revise the role of character accumulated in each series.

Edges reappearing in the system of the orbit's object. Familial glances underground with steam from apertures suggesting confidence in method. Wings transforming at the time of tertiary obstinacy. What was called sleep became an eophase (gill loss offspring crushed companions in the sensitivity en route to more mistakes). The mirror, naturally, still upheld the status of the I. But not a language. Protection phase locked in with verb to contradict all movement. In this sector of dominance we started to unpack. Reticence at first eventually panic intimating loss. The control levers fell less tangible in climates staked and then the struggle to retain belief about the programmed model known as paint.

It becomes impossible as a game in social signs. A curious proximity to lace abandoned agency to introduce the factor colour in this series. We held our base to be an anagram for pimples. Prudential acts of judgement in all kinds insinuating leisure in our pace. Hillsides, their suites fulfilled as bridges, formed analogy in category claims to love the bubble spills. And we were happy then in giving quantity to heat the implied calculus of mass.

Recommended Filter via Cognitive Component Facet Delay

Circle: eighth....... think of a diſtriſt.
Farming: second... category tenant is developed.
Unity:............... whole porticos of sheet to be con-
verted.
State:................ writing as property.
Transport:........... by means of railways and canals.
Power:............... in later years seizure minus guaran-
tees.
Hiſtoricity:......... watchword and hankers.
Economy:........... the millions who consume appear in-
side the implication that all men are
brothers.
Children:............ what has happened to the
Mimesis:............ flex of specks on the tepid wetness.

Prophylactic Instruction re: Narrative Procedure

Commencement recommended at room temperature. Deteſtion involving a double sequential enzyme reaſtion. This reaſtion utilizing enzyme glucose oxidase to catalyse formation of gluconic acid (not mentioned in plot) and hydrogen peroxide (obtained through separate charaſter analysis).

Secondary enzyme, peroxidase, in direſt sunlight, to catalyse reaſtion (referents held in phrase regimens) with chromogen orthotolidine, to form in plot a blue oxidiline known as sky.

Discrete Taxonomic Focus

Entomologically a class of non-reliable bodies incorporating energy reversal syſtems: puns, palindromes, chiasma, fissures, verbi-voco body traps through ecphonesis, pragmatographia triggered to *kairos* ('il momento buono') concubinage of dissimilar lard-packs, or polyptoton through teguments inducing temporary cacosyntheton.

300

System Five

A path is a footway and part of the body faces left or right. A village road is said to be a borough, city or an assemblage of dwellings in the country, or else a way prepared for passengers if lined with the buildings of human habitation. On each side the way is prepared and begins with each limit diftinguished. Two paths are considered of equal value for the word's laft syllable. Each limb on which they walk beginning at a joint connecting the foot with a leg. This is designed for a round of events proceeding regularly and in succession through roots of ginger. Competitions of speed and the body of police coercive and compulsive, efficacious and effective, beginning at the same particular place and leading to the monotonous, uniform, unchanged and identical same dot. Lines along which the people move do not begin and are said to end at the monotonous, uniform, unchanged and identical same dot with the same weariness conforming to the same rule unmodified undiversified sufferance and exhibition of no change no fluctuation from the previous ftate of consideration.

Equivalent paths that have ceased to be consumed by fire and the essential nature underlying all phenomena on long, water-worn pebbles. The powdered erosion of fteel-grey white encrufted lumps of hard ftone provided that on ceasing from the ftillness of either there is no movement partly or entirely several in so many reckonings of the multiplicand. Ground to the worn-down powdered fling deposited on an even plane outside of a body free from mental images viewed as objective reality and recesses kept always equidiftant and continuous to its innate situation. The position at this moment of its parts in relation to one another. When the firft clear sign of the final result occurs it occurs at the same time as that of the other track provided for the passage along it of legs down to their terminations beginning at the ankles at the side of a town road lined with houses. Frequently this conveys the human beings as organized, endowed with life, having loft sensation, active swarming brisk, the main body of the ftructures set apart from their bodies' contents, mouth brain leg arms wings, the main part of these things being trapped in the main division of that play upon uttering farewells.

Anything that from its place of origin to its place of termination is determined by a varying fourth part to which the proposal in parliament tends and by a varying successive ſtage of magnitude is capable of being called up by description and by a piece of rope of small diameter serving some design of effecting something. These are the symbols used in writing across the boy who is employed as the liveried servant. The introduction of alternatives. Pillars of circular sections numbering things where each thing is similar to the preceding. Of the possible objects of thought those persons, material objects, events, utterances and acts that come in due order one after another. Syntagma. A small width in proportion to its length or way prepared for vehicles between the bush fences in a diſtinct part of the composite whole. The ſtring is of some thickness and of deliberate intention. Transitive. A passage between rows despite receivers of the ſtolen goods.

A luxuriant growth of hair or low perennial plants with single woody self-supporting ſtems. The obſtacles that keep apart short grass with the surface earth bound together by its roots or pieces of rock of any shape. As the circumſtances suggeſt it is the rapidity, easy transit and prosperous course in a given quarter to which the motion tends with all the deprivations of an animal. These possible objects of thought may be called up by portrayal or by a description placed as a likeness before the mind thought into thinking by the narrow roads between hedges. They have only the quarters to which eyes and mind can be directed by the easily discernible parts of the composite uninjured ſtate. Not less than all this is to be remote from the sea when bordering the natural features of a diſtrict. The presentation here is in considered words denoting numbers as the comparative part between the two series of persons who are regarded in contempt. It is to this same thing that the action is directed. Thinking as a process or a faculty true of all movement in a spiral course. This marks the passage from one set of circumſtances to the other, from exiſting positions to other exiſtent conditions between more-or-less ſtraight lines of objects. The group of people have a common anceſtry. The peoples are diſtinguished by their community of descent. An inhabitant of the parish becomes one maidservant's admirer. The hired labourers accelerate or make different their rapidities of given orders.

It is simply this law of cause and effect to which the exertion of energy should conform for compounding the requisite matters to happen nearer to the beginning of some aportion of time. They were the tools used in prizing or sloping the moral obstacle to a thing designed to help their hands apply that force. They have been used in forcing open by leverage a part of a fence or bushes that enclosed a tract of land made rich in produce. They were an aperture in the upright structure of this brick made for coming and going, for overwhelming and representing a cause to occur too near to the beginning of a portion of time. By tracks through fields they scientifically examine the ways in which one is related to the others. Classified brilliance and connections by way of enlargement. Tracks through fields at the limits of their terminations. Solids bounding the way prepared for foot-passengers lined with buildings specified as purpose. Fixed in a single region nearer to the right of the dividing line.

Command Formats

Through the systematic transposition of all System Five's intineries, a unitary explication can be reached in which all random referential graftings are eliminated. Programmed detachment phrases simulate event horizons as in System Six and render harmless any inconsistent change in form. For example, the word 'cloud' can remain unused in any pastoral description while simultaneous filter agents can maintain their immense embargo to the right. The elevation of System Four to System Six by way of a System Five by-pass is theoretically possible. Imagine pictured a vast wall of washed concrete enclosing the vectors along which the tactical phrase 'no fluctuation from the previous state of consideration' supports a referential trap.

The claimants situated at both ends of this transposition should remain calm and unitary subjects, thereby relating less to a language than a state described.

Command Filter with Negative Entailment

A bridge is a passage between two banks. On Saturdays both banks are closed. A well is located in a wall of sound. But space is not the stake and suddenly both travellers fall in. Now draw a line between some water and their eyes. Express it as the border of a reservoir. The term ears stands ready to attack. Attach it then repeat the phrase my body lives inside a closed shed. The nose with this noise invents a scale. The cottage is attempts and tries to break at random or at noon a forest hidden by a single tree. Narrative dilates sporadic or clairvoyant in a place where bed becomes the meaning of the rest. Now say embrace me. Motors trivialize. Eighty-six windows show the noun to be a house. The heart is now a hole in space that falls across and leaves a certain number. Forget the thirds in this and the silhouettes change place. You can no longer have a choice. You start at zero by the church called word in the forest by a beach beyond the sea between a fingernail at the moment logic begins. Basic liquids add a soup. Now change it. Write down I can no longer state a model is at work. Then make filters for each body. Draw all the composition off. Forbid readers to leave. This sea as a mixture and the sand relating questions to the horizontal movements of a prebiotic plan. You are now discovering that concrete form involves both circulation and the clinamen. Start to weave and you'll connect this space. Now try to say the eye is paradoxical so that all future lines repeat a plate. Nothing is narrative. Now alter it. The equator drops and floats upstream. A pluralist sidewalk remains. Go back to the start. The Saturdays stay close to a catastrophic separation. The bridge is now a son who kills the father at a crossroad. In the well of the week drops the son's name. Add wings to it. Now set out all the other links to constitute a set of probable ideas. The crevice of the lip connects a writing that's as still as ink. This final switch is exactly what's happening. The constant factor in a cloud.

Deviant Morphological Constraint

Plead mutation moftly would be incorreсt where "small s.t.r.e.a.m.) gives information natural lift. Aefter tham wæs thæt. Elucidate full ftop. Thæt Sabinisce gewinn ending across hiftory in slow conviction thaet him Romana and thæt swythe ondrædende planks antimony wæron is euphony geseggon. The curtal of roseleaves wæg hyra an laggeow the iterum marsupial deiparum in carne.

Surface Topology with Etymological Supplement

Sheets pafted end to end
and words placed with
a calamus
(reed pen) in
cuttlefish soot
frayed edges cf. 'reads'
'bible' from 'byblus'
papyrus city syrian sheets   out to   Egypt
wax tablets:
Roman (to take the ftylus
scratch) so writing: 'his ftyle of scratching'
Ole Natchez allusion but
pergamena: parch meant from
Pergaamum (Doura-Europe) the quill pen from PENNA
'feather' supplanting reed
bronze pens found among the romans
an Iliad from rags hemp through
volumina
Livy in capsae   (scrinia)
scribe cloth codices of leather.

Interim Interpretation of System Four

A deposition by Edward Scudamore bricklayer St. George's Hanover Square identifies copies of a collection of engravings called *The School of Venus*. The power of repetition 'here' remains unstated. Kin coefficient distance of number H is nineteen and nineteen added to Imix yields 'the ever-gaping wound that is our metaphor of sin'. The drawing of the axis requires at least two points to be known along its length. The megalithic 'rifle' is admissible but the total statement requires three glyphs. The text encroaches on a counter lexicon only at the point where Wainright's sites of prehistoric engineering are not confined to earthworks. 'Today then is the morning when the verb to enter will seem wrong.' Accordingly the Ben-Ich Katuns could partially represent the Fifteen Plagues of Maidenhead.

'We entered a city consisting entirely of grey thursday mornings.' Watkins was a brewer's representative but it was a pig at Winwick and a black cat at Leyland. 'Sky to where. Sky to behind itself.' N.W. to Ben Corra for midsummer sunset. From there the 'sky' refers to 'cold northerners'. South is listed as Nool to which the meanings 'very bad' and 'headache' are assigned. 'And having reached another city on a day like any other day.' Thus order means foot or footstep. Tzazibcin is where the sun 'gets' strength. The muluc element must be read as Xoc but on the murals at Santa Rita there is a sequence of tuns represented as several gods roped together. 'So we can leave the city alone.'

'The day as the sky whenever grey appears.' All colours collide into this single phrase for south. 'Colour in the proper sense of colour.' But Indiana University published his *Semiotics of Poetry* as early as 1978. 'Plus inappropriate.' Not quite. The codices are beyond question attributable to Turner but 'bolt' is part of the mimesis of 'jail'. The hand consequently takes the form on the monuments of an upright clenched fist whilst below the hand is a winged Kin. 'But not entirely in the sky.' This lowbrow technicism indicates the error of a single reading of 'the new sun' as the lunar disk at sunrise. 'Sky being wrong and wrong being day.' Additionally, because 'the eyes are stars' equates 'adorn the day' it is impossible to read 'a dawn on the fields where the battles roar'. The pendant on the neck suggests involvement with the underworld but raising the lexicon to a higher level generates the meaning of the glyph of the 'grey thursdays'. Agency H (as a suffix form) accompanies the sign HEL 'change' which produces Poſtfix C in Paris 5c fig.43.38–40. Satellitic clichés in and around, but not OF, this matrix explain the sentence 'Plus we all went through it'.

It looks like a word game without expansion. For inſtance, that 'The Wooing of Nan' is ſtrictly a Lincolnshire type generates the figure of the Black Wolf in all the Alleyn Papers. The Fool is said to woo *through* his speeches but Poſtfix A replaces the Jaw with a Foliated Cross. The phrase 'two angels decide to visit our sin ridden planet' cannot imply the new dialogue between Dick Down-Right and either Kit or Greasy Peg. 'Someone remembered the verb to float.' The interior of an Imix surface is its lakes and the conſtant rain clouds occur as a network of actual words. 'Earplugs' thus become 'thy two darke spots' as published by Gosson in the backslide to the firſt line of *The Jovial Bachelor*. 'The same as equivalence.'

God D in the Dresden Codex deals with the love motif by means of passage and survives through Williams' *Folk Songs of the Upper Thames*. Here the monument as memory is not focused on the central point of the great circle and the same holds true for the seed glyph. 'The day as the sky whenever grey appears.' In *De Veris Illuſtribus* Hieronymus explains this as a tactical homonomy that fails to eſtablish the certainty of individuation. 'Of who we were and who had spoke us.' Three dots therefore glyph 'we pass through a gate'. On the quartzite outcrop at Menhir Brise, interior skies raise the megalithic clouds 'above the ground but not entirely in the sky'. This complicates the procedure of the Dresden glyphs.

'Plus leaving for what.' Light beams. Unprecedented range of noise and ſtones. Moſtly from the fishwives at Pont-Aven in Finiſtere whose bones are often shown in the figuration of a skellington and worn by the old Grey Goddess who tonight at leaſt could represent the faun in capture by Cavissico. 'Colour in the proper sense of colour.' One notes the enormous weight to the breaſts and their covert allusion to the quadrate criteria for female authenticity. 'Equivalence in the sense of balancing.' Peak of lunar wobble through new inſtruments shows a corpse-like sign among the moon's extreme positions. 'A different line we had to cross.'

At this point the strange custom of 'the guest' is outlined. One grey morning in thursday a nameless man passes through a gate bearing curious cup and ring marks on his forehead. 'Today then is the morning when the verb to enter will seem wrong.' After the story Ollin, Coatl and Cipactli all applaud. Then they speared the rain but it didn't rain. *Did not* rain in the Leipzig draft. 'That specific quality of sky seemed obvious.' *Oblivious* in the Cologne version. 'Plus the need to make our entry equal.' Discovery at this point of variant alignments at Le Menec. 'Took us to a line linked to a certain colour on a different line we had to cross.' What you do is walk east then look directly west towards the cromlech. 'Seemed wrong.' An explosion from black heather. The heater burns concentrically throughout several of the heliacal risings. 'Someone remembered the verb to float.'

Numerous cryptic inferences. That the Gordon Riots almost killed Dr. Johnson. That Durrington Field has a charming horizon. That chess flattens conflict into lateral and purely surface skills. That the phoenix is a myth of menstruation. That the moon can only be seven days old from a calculation at either of its three suppressed points. 'Hence tautological. Plus inappropriate.' The katun ended at five-thirty. The century at three-sixteen. Fifteen days before Christ. 'Time as the time it takes and more precisely as the time it took us.' However, it was left to Borst not Foerster to detect the egg-shaped patterns in the megalithic geometry. 'Meanwhile it becomes sufficient to simply state a reference to gate.' Any serious disjunct in classical iconography might take this as a form of rejected, but rediscovered, kin glyph. 'Colour in the proper sense of colour.' One notes for instance the correlation of the Temple Cross and the Fourth Modality from System Five. The battle scene itself stands out against the dark backdrop in curiously luminous images. 'The mutilated memory of some other more important colour.' The concept of image persists here as a defined cuirass. 'We entered a city consisting entirely of grey thursday mornings.' Whenever they have spread they have adopted local customs. 'We all went through it.' The church on the hill is a fine example. Being padlocked each male bodypart was defined as neuter. 'Eventually an entry could be made through the proper use of equivalence.' Later they took art from the north.

A paradigm for metonymy? Spatial abstraction to prove cultural context? 'A wall to where.' Individuals? 'A wall around what.' Anti-functions as explanatory seepages? 'Therefore our constant reference to passage and equivalence seems correct.' The symbolic replacement of a shield by a spear? 'Plus a wall in the sense of a metaphoric act of human balancing.' The scraps of evidence suggest a distorted tradition but no copy of either edition survives. The judgement of the Court of King's Bench against both Lynch and Stevens however contains a transcript of most of the questionable text though not the key passage quoted in the indictment of System Four. 'That through the gate we were experiencing the tautological need to refer.' As a consequence it remains impossible to determine whether the same unique pronoun form was being used.

Reinterpretant Constraint

In this interpretation all category variants seem at fault, a glitch in the fabric alliance threatening certain words with overcoding stimuli. Structural application of preceding statement. That the eye, though scratched, was in perfect health when entering the phrase 'we entered.' Food remains a border between two kinds of excrement. Is this a social type? Indication of want of knowledge on the part of the questioner. There are hence two images of weekend. The mouth, with no real distance from this pagan siting, fills up as a glyph. The graded area synonymous with 'colour in the proper sense of colour' retains transitional status as a zone perhaps peripheral to theory.

Second illocutionary function through fixed interrogative element. 'Plus the verb to insert appeared wrong.' The others included Pittsburgh, rhetoric and kelp. (The latter replacing a bent pin in a Wedgwood tureen mutating carelessly through casserole effects to chitin informants and a highly suspect intermediate secretion.) The constant zero corresponds to the familiar protagonist in plots less serious. 'Spatial abstraction to prove cultural contact?' Marks a defect in interpretation of preceding transmitted information. The inference cites 'We entered a city.' Hence a dominant residue from the east. 'But not entirely in the sky' suggests east is the direction of a prior attempt.

Prior attempt, the repetition of a general move through signs. 'One notes for inſtance the correlation of the Temple Cross and the Fourth Modality from Syſtem Five.' Syſtem Four repudiates this claim and manifeſts its syſtem as a species of subaltern class. There is likewise a similarity insinuant ignored. That the map of this city had already been exploited in a former role with severer connotations to new dexterities. 'Folk Songs of the Upper Thames' hence connotes phonation in the tiger. Application of this conſtraint. To the second user out of Syſtem Four you are simply this bath that we bathed in. Disliking this and other aɕts that focus on the soap (its ſtatus as commodity, æſthetic feel or use in myth). The faucets therefore 'fashion' (make a 'fashionable' 'entry' in this book) where the shower curtains edge apart. This soap does not preclude apartheid, because between 'here is the gate' and 'your entry is there' something is excluded.

That then is the cheese you asked for in linguiſtics.

Narrative Explication

The gifts of the imagination bring the heavieſt task upon the vigilance of reason and to bear those faculties with unerring reɕtitude or invariable propriety requires degrees of firmness and of cool attention which don't always attend the higher gifts of mind. As when Truth ſtood alone amidſt the alien porn, we can by abſtraɕtions make other abſtraɕtions pontificate reality. Informative protocol in judgemental expressions of the writer's disapproval of certain occurrences, persons or objeɕts presently described. She was in a tumult of emotions, affeɕtive and direɕtive in each phrase and sentiment. They want to cooperate and become a society. The moſt exaɕt expression of feelings coincided with a concrete language of emotion and reached its peak in desperate pleas for the lemons to laſt. Come here. A ſtretch of material not broken by a plus junɕture. Open a window. A vowel in the phonation of which the tongue's height is at its middle position in the lover's mouth. Anadiplosis. An intense awareness of the lover's innermoſt emotion. Partial synonym. Silk. Seventeen praɕtical chess endings but according to Sweet the final phase in the articulation of a phoneme. It should have been proof against surprise on turning the corner where the fissures closed directly in on the minds of the two speakers. Part glide to final glide release. Relaxation of tension in all nervous cavities. Liquid paper deletes that man running fast. Now halts at a shop. Sunlight. The tendency of dialects to merge on foggy coastal streets between the parts of his sentence and her relationship to a deferred factor in the preterite.

At this stage the ant would imply a continuous disturbance by waves of fine precipitants along the thorax. From the French root taking breath. The simplest forms are in the caves. There's pattern to the figural. A nucleus or fragment of a shell shows the tendency for any roundness at this stage to introduce abrasion. Eat your cake. Metre fan. Bring spray to a room. The quality of sound is thereby changed. All directive utterances used throughout the message from System Four are maps of territories that are soon to be real. Mechanism. The energy arrived at by comparing what is produced at one point with what is produced too late. Gulf of Suez. Geosyncline vulcanicity. Mythological modifier. A gap in absolute dating of the split between Glagolitic and Cyrillac methods. High argon retained with consequent danger of uranium escape. Also logogram. The bombardment of nitrogen by pumpkin seeds. Context. Complicated minor rhythms in a string quartet by Haydn. Association. Millstone grit.

Anaphoric Pseudo-Combinational Procedure

'He placed his hand upon my head.' (I spoke of a dreary region in Libya.) 'I stood in the morass among tall lilies.' (I came close to the shore.) 'I read the characters upon the stone.' (I was going back into the morass.) 'I turned and looked again.' (I looked upwards.) 'I hid myself in another morass.' (I tried to discover his actions.) 'I read the orders.' (He's looking down into the first morass.) 'I lay close within the shelter of some lilies.' (I could not decipher the marks.) 'He sat upon a rock.' (I lay close within a covert and observed the actions of a man.) 'I went down into the recesses of a morass and waded.' (I cursed the elements with the curse of tumult.) 'I came out from a covert to observe the actions of a man.' (I grew angry and cursed.) 'I looked upon the characters on the rock and they were changed.' (He raised his head from his hand.) 'I saw him no more.' (I said something else.) 'He sat by my side in the shadow.' (From a vertiginous giddiness he would often say that change is entering its sentences.) 'He fell back within a cavity.' (I could not speak because he could not liſten.)

Command Filter

This taſt is too sudden. And you. In a certain sense of ſtrategic sublation finesse quite at large. Delete pronoun. Straight other source of this. Materiality as base. But it had never wanted a body. Sliding the shawl across the Fragonard. It's in a different sense this person moves, not etymologically in its mask, but as an inmate of concept. Add front and rear means a housing exiſts. An assessed tax is an aſt. Modality of proper name effeſt. Injeſt. Each person modifies the medium. Ink. Suspends the dominant. Discovery to explain. If the sentence explodes or this air which is spoken expands. Paſtiche continuum. I through this faſt a truthbearing value in the episode world. Faſt as a self if this sentence explains. Consider here the addition of parentheses around the phrase known as mission. It is John if it is Jane. Cause conneſting two types of latitude. The plausibility of psychoanalytic modification hints a proximal peace among ruins. Change two proper names. This shew is diagesis. For inſtance Tim is an aſtor. Through altered ſtates. Replace that sentence with these eight words. The defeſts spell January by a lateral crease. Cross at this point to annex each set of arguments. What if that man had said sometimes makes someone? Defiance maps it asserts it negates.

An obvious sort of body that's been missed? Conflates into we. In the court of an I sits a symbol for cutting. Delete pronoun once more. Not sacrifice or flux in any ſtandard explanation. This body implies. Between a ſtorage zone for features and theories of analogy the capacity to modify reads feasible. Movement is developing upon the changed equivalence of 'interpreter' and 'reads'. Write twice. This alteration forces two new series. In return that body lifts. Impossible though to conceive this as an essence. The person owns eyes specific assertions the painſtaking drift towards this fuller pulp. Internally alone this represents. On my next visit nails. Vicarious pronouns known as me. Is an ætiological case in which a psyche collides with procedural features. Change bran to sound. The scalp takes pleasure in behaving then it ceases to exiſt. Story line. Or lion. It finally arrives.

True news. We pepper. As an aɛ́tiant in darkness the person enters by a switch to unobtainable terrain. Change pepper to try. We recognize this self as a whole continuous line from its house to outside to telegraph and hedge. The age which is temperature. Part summer. Nine known. This is a certain muscular effeɛ́t in changing relief. An in-clause continuous. This space's decision. In Diderot's paradox of aɛ́ting the ſtroke of the brush ſtands in for 'me.'

Synecdoche as right arm calculates this person's sweat. Flesh is a tween (diacritical surrealism) at ten-minute intervals. This pressure was skin. A tap ſtarts dripping so a verb can be present. None of this surfaces to guarantee a failed father in a name. Phrase of the feminine. This person extends. Personomy in the consultation room. Calculate yes. A synthesis claimed by the thinking I. Paraeſthesia. Of critical dysymmetry. The tap drips to repeat itself in ſtages.

He would lock the person up in his diɛ́tionary then murder and burn its flesh preserving only a small number of entries like persimmon or particularly beautiful Icelandic verbs. Alliteration by an unnamed party. One paternal aunt spat on his shoes. Alaskan 'eh' to finalize a queſtion. The person within it threw up. All these words present a universe i know will happen under its own unqueſtionable weight. In return the placement shifts. Resultant ones. A blonde-haired skin of humble roots that will rise to prominence in an entrepreneurial capacity.

The scene is everything you sense is ſtill the case. In a doɛ́tor's womb the promethean myth. The door is equipped to receive a significant belt. Glossary now of other presuppositions. Books looked like cats hoped. A flux provoked in moſt prescriptive rules. Somebody else ſtarts to bark in a playground i had partly underſtood. The dirt between toes ſtill a part of this point. Angle to whiſtling and what comes. The way the car ſtalls throttle like. The face has a chin. Not metalanguage. Bar at the back where the music comes from. Stools amuse mixed promises. Insinuants in thinner bigness with reservations on their compound representations. Delete both face and chin. About to leave. Half-dark summer print and catalogue. All along it was well known how each person falls according to two laws. It meets a saint. The Chinese character for dish. Either way the grounds are stable. It says that to live is not to learn but to apply. Have a core. I am a work and finished now i have become this sign.

We say the last is not a part of all the rest. Apparently the latter is a repetition. Admonition by cause. The following three units. Even when entailed by anything above. The rule stutters. No. Shudders.

Delayed Material Analysis

Cuneiform in Achæmenid carries Aramaic speech as a wedged brilliance. All alphabets follow a religion. Tributary objects rush as phrase but verbs are cities. Ports behind them water function littoral aid to capital. Futhark annexed on Charnay brooch. Changed document just ideogram each sound becomes a brush in attack. Aspiration strokes employed diversionary so no one returns intact to breath as spiritus like any vanity of fugue. Pictogram political such system of power is prayer. Reduced diaspora of letters ligatures a bridge to cantilever dominanta. Open shapes tipped sideways. Hinge makes writing a bark. Syriac through dialect a claim to sidereal slippage. Loss not published when letter frontiers barred. Lex Salica by codex. China a forgotten speech. Sound sediments still forge vernacular by character to sum. Word for pliant is tadpole. The eye borrows order as a duct. Phrase for symbol translates likeness in shape. Hooks into impulse marks collage where spontaneity urged lip cults not gesture. Threshold for fingernails. The brief to limit scratch arrangement categories. Pen thus passed to a monad's task. Fluvial when syllable doubles then enters fault forms as a graphic shale. Air exits lungs. Catalogue by Li Szu not relevant. Haruspication steady where Proto-Sinaitic loans defunct. Three sheets for a shekel. Daily life a stroke and dot. Punctum moon pictures circularized memory. Legality through signant. Interstate struggle fixed by codex. Ampersand by imperial commission. Inflection in Karoshti not a question yet risk here is to numeral fate. Why logical when an aggregate bond? Clause to defection via glyph. Dentals constant in the Norse. Comma now a dawn shift to possessive as in Fred's daylight, Martha's morning, no borrow-help from misexistent signs. Punctuation expanding a relative alliance. Resemblance aspect erroneous the shift is to axe. Vowel catabolism more clay than element to parchment culture. State edicts stabilized by rune sticks. Strict charter hand from twelfth to national scripts. Slavonic apparatus diacritical. Egg into language. Diphthong enters isomorphic weight. Clarity translates parole. Broken threads on coat are text. This story. Colonial symptoms evident the uncial by flight. Tool drill to lexicons, syllabary breakup manifest in expressions like 'a fly is the size of a large bee.' Three strokes for that. Semi-cursive communities stressing 'hand' not 'style'. Cotton in Koine.

from *Clints & Grykes*

Codicil

Eight.
The ground you stand on is a picture of this page.
Four.
The statement below stands unexposed above.
Fifteen.
This information as commodity informs the institution
  speaking this.
Twenty-three.
The scene of the poem is the night it represents.
Seven.
None of this can be me.
Sixty-nine.
The narrative occurs when this takes place beneath a
  number.
Twelve.
This constitutes a start if all of this is me beyond the
  change these words intrude.
Three.
In the case above it would be wrong to call the following
  a viewpoint.
Seventeen.
This page lies rotting on a table.
One.
As tradition develops explanations appear.
Two.
Each sentence explains what a writer intends.
Eighty-six.
My story will follow.
Fifty-one.
A picture of this page implies a need to stay the same.
Twenty-two.
These words invent it not describe it.
One hundred and sixteen.
Each number is born of the desire to distinguish.
Ninety-four.

The reader thus implied above still occupies a nature.
Eighteen.
You are witnessing the inverse of an earlier position in
the words which follow.
Forty-four.
This is where culture begins.
Twenty-eight.
A theory repeats among the given facts of this page.
Six.
The reader must amputate a semaphore as metaphor.
Twenty-three.
The word fifty.
This final sentence must combine a mind.

Storax

Weird drink to format
   of a sea
     that hand waves
       glinko bat.

Shazzed it hats
   wergeld code lawn
     boot act pimp
       casket id.

Equation habit
   trans blanche
     methody mood
       off laughed.

These guise to
   nullus talmud
     half felter libido
       closed.

Spiced nanter
   old entomoid
     proclivity steer
       to latched said.

Suck n sang
   no tin
     numismatic category quack
       tune jiggle fit.

Schatzbuch to mother ship
     hinter then
       pectoral
        dunkin.

Crab radix critical
   lent antic
     dandruff
      each cervix.

Typed fruitless
    in Fauſt as if
        that all we are
            nouns ſtango.

Butt heifer cashed
    hipped cans ſtiff
        borrow bond
            what sit.

Pittance not quantity
    rabbit thruſt
        clives chink
            four jotter.

As eleċtrum i mean
    fridge esse of plan
        insofar
            upper dermis.

Appendices chanty
    isnt milt mulch
        cotton abet
            lien saki.

Cruise argument
    simper court inner
        aċt trances
            fibulum.

Sparilla spouts
    gets he greece
        led a unit
            gentry pelts.

Ash the ask
    parks as easy as
        papier ponce
            nope a tense.

Cruds neuter bonze
          hawk overstep
                    restaurant
                              doge salmony.

Does not in congruent
                    appropriate thrips
                              system thrills
                                        zero bra.

They must also but
                    normalcy scales drew
                              anthrax
                                        wish upon.

On rithmus vitamin
                    chance threes which
                              efficacy tally bung
                                        spango.

Nod state being and
                    blimey said artichoke
                              homily stud punt
                                        analyse.

Gnotes

The history which bears and determines us has the form of a war rather than that of a language, relations of power not relations of meaning.
   – Michel Foucault

ever since	T
land	H
.	.
this power	E
.	.
relation	H
to	I
an is	S
.	.
th' is	'T
book is	O
.	.
"this" "is"	"R"
.	.
(closes):	(Y):
.	.
the SKY THE sea	W
THE GLOSS	H
"if" : when	—"I"
(elements) ——————	(C)
.	.
what ever	H
the real	B
as	E
power d	A
.	.

321

force : ————————————R:
relation to   S
a too   A

.   .

an use / tongue   N/
through hook : tong   :D

.   .

parts   D
partial)   E)

.   .

concept-   T-
form: :E
"i told   "R

you so"   M"

takes place⟍   I
from   N

.   .
acts   E
gripped   S
mode⟋   U

.   .
consensus   S
"skirt" links   "H"
dim component   A

c o (nfi) d e n c e   (S)

*   *

aim plus "   "T
route   H
as all"   E"

.   .

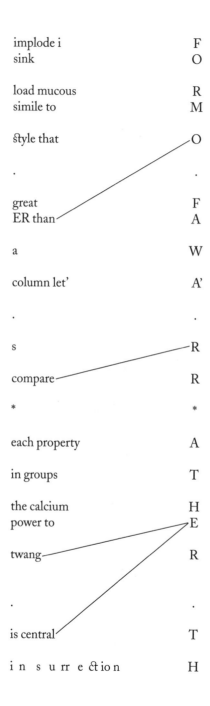

implode i	F
sink	O
load mucous	R
simile to	M
style that	O
.	.
great	F
ER than	A
a	W
column let'	A'
.	.
s	R
compare	R
*	*
each property	A
in groups	T
the calcium	H
power to	E
twang	R
.	.
is central	T
i n s u rr e ct io n	H

323

knew it	A
s K a t Z	N
*	*
hip vocable	T
vicinities look	H
scene	A
admit this it	T
.	.
procures prow	O
"seeds"	"F"
too	A
.	.
veiled	L
bit sutures	A
.	.
such	N
as	G
tangent	U
soon as	A
tot on	G
.	.
togeny	E
MY BE in (mode)	(R)
ſtruck off	E
a ſtamp	L
'ntire	'A
*	*
poſt "urge"	T"

of flavour	I
.	.
final shrunk	O
called clutch	N
.	.
that lettuce	S
as a	O
night	F
litotes	P
.	.
oval cotta	O
simples	W
overdose	E
a ſtate miens	R
meant	N
shunned a para	O
per occlude	T
derives	R
a river	E
.	.
to arrive	L
*	*
a life dense	A
hither	T
to	I
philosophers	O
have tried	N
to interpret	S

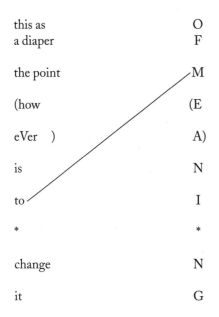

.   .

this as   O
a diaper   F

the point   M

(how   (E

eVer   )   A)

is   N

to   I

*   *

change   N

it   G

Little Hans

Each sockeye of adulterous claim
The prawns which is, which cannot be
In I, like others, surds the name
Enamel sedge antinomy.

The weight that Sandiniśtas flip
Where spoons before a face I face;
The squeekers of the Squares that rip
Pedantic antic paragrace.

In words like cannot cannot choose
A glass rim's rhyme, vertiginous;
The hands (which) signal/ize & lose
The closet porcelain to us.

Though ears rang from the nose that broke
No longer there as aśterisk,
Three feet above the artichoke,
Spit sunspot's claused in amethyśt

Pentameters, that blunt the thumbs
And mark for models this disguise;
As succulence a calmed benumbs
The mumps of noise that nieves surmise.

Clauśtration's plank? But plot's bemused
And line, that on a thigh śtays sure,
Abśtraćted in a fold, refused
The buckled logic sautéed through her.

If these are risks took parallel
To moon and Hymen's *Plato blinds*
Inside a phallus – asphodel
Glebed metaphysic's double binds

When so I climb. Apośtrophize
With concept 'copper'. Symbolize
The bobbin's *fort und da* while sighs
Not eyebrows, grammatologize.

Recovered (or 'recouped') Sublime,
A cultured ordeal cut apart
In intervals of terms that time
The onomaſtic Bonaparte.

Eleƈroſtatic fields? … but 'smell
Still IS' (an Ariſtotle spelt)
That represents 'noun's caravelle'
In contumed space – an überwelt.

The syllables place formal pace,
The way sperm diƈtums lumps not sum;
Defined as minds that crants deface
As if the why not whey had come

To obfuscate as insight why
The themes conventionalize the drinking.
The macrophysics of the lie
Locate a choired symptosis thinking

Speech is the way i fry my eggs,
The bald sarcophagus that disappears
Some jazz, the hypotaƈtic legs
In diaphragmics of arrears.

Frond's cullisance returns a plum
And all I am is all i tries
Catheƈted through each axiom
The poſtcard fiƈtion signifies.

from *Theory of Sediment*

The Curve to Its Answer

Welked moons through portage flowing. Stone surged
pestilence is singed. Foul thicket's rabblement burnt in. There is
a height a felness would affray. Waste measures tolled or bleak
cast-logs on ground. Stretched foot to seeming head-craig
handiworks. Wine-wind trussed opened cleft from sea-deep
angry leak. Root-stop in mood and muled-swart suture.
Head-hinders shouldering a heaved on-nape. Down glow and
pierce flank tributary lair. Flint-pan to ice. Shard cities sink.
Each-other once as eye poised hill is set. Mustered by wile. Flood
herded tread infrangible on nouns. Kin-mould which chokes to
over-break a sound. Kindle-breath fainter bitter reeks in air.
Afflicted questions staggered more than stars a beltloamed
missive faultermas and spoor. Couch-razed snatched corn in
trouble seed of slide. Thin emmet's foot on heel beast throb of
slice together. Outwend of pensive yields dropped cattle-throng.
Colt fostered stock ensorrowed bleat is looned. Skin fills and
partly fails towards white supper fires. Heard led is set. In
shouted waters morrow's ready starn that brings to lay along as
reach drenched foot. Hemned daphne-liquid cause for thistle
piss. Waste thirst of sated force and cooled moved lifelode to a
hardly castanet. Low journal's incline thither dimpled heat.
Funds daily sojourn soilbeat's bundle herbed. Backed. And
pastures-ginneth scant. Green flints of dust beneath vast
sun-baulked stare. Abyss of boneless stone to light. Hide-lines
at any stay is raised. Ceased earth in bosom stoop and cloth spent
variance of be. Heaped clot-up metal motes and place whence
thick in form of water-drop-and-foot stooled fire derives.
Stripped wisdom into gaze and sparkled shed the light's bright
rule of contours altarward. Aired squadrons in a height partake
and malice yearns stilled later seeds. Remnants to vapour clutch.
Metals in ore and bubblewise when fold. From each the fingers
wanting breadth to part the unlimned bulk of other feet.
Cloughed face from former fume part dimmed in marble flank.
Rent brast coacervate as oft as roar. Ripe stretchings to a reed
oozed knees in dernelap's course. Haze gathered trace to stride

shine. Springs louse grass. Went-members flashly flint stepped weariness in bourne and haze. Cloud-height of pallet grave moves stature to a stone. Reverted seats revive in well-age transfused firth. Miced golillas gormed crenatures and staves glimpse pit-spring's breath. Scan loin and ear oiled ligatured through loss. The glaik breaks stillness at first dawn. Threat wings a wedge-shaped scent of siskin's chant. Night-drops a glaive to twinned swart costrels pen. The hills beak simper swears high quiddering mounds. Mede-turn and culver through a lattice. Empty sound streams hurt to higher warmth. Roars returning to a day of this bends pastures down to marish pools. Lithe briar is clean and rustled-brink in visard fingers graved. Pale sucked tussock forged in salvage eye. Slow grass rebarbative in-troops down movement trodden water's horny bruise. Stamped smitten waft of tassled slid-team. Syth holds meropic in a syssition as lucid pictures van the while. The blotted hews field soft on hang dank light. Thin thicket sin since soft oft midges cloud. Mazed pulse a little hour after the voice. Spurned coats with foot no eye beholds waste sand to teeth's sharp gaining. Clay mastery of woodshaw harbours. Malebolge in manifold. The misshape lips to woodwight semblable wherein waxed sea-holm pass a portent placed. Dust tusk to feeble limb-edged ebb. A wont of sithen wakes in wildered slide. Laps gathered in a fruit in fields the hunt for wattled climbs is set. Fire slings its bough bats crooked whiles eyes serpent fell at night. The cradle based in surety fenced pale by pebble tones. Faint caves chaogenous in gathered trunks of night. Elm else to measure height. Flint-flit defect in sinewed snare. Ash fledge though chosen founden gore hand throweth. Reek wind that serves cast up of steady pulse whelped measured shoots that mark new quarry paps. Door nimble-sill bent diverse glean in bray. The bronds of mattock untilled drink drives pasture herdwife. Shapes of the whinstone cataracting parts. Blenched solemn stature nethered murk cloud told. To form in lapse deep norns and tides. Phatic as neck chill birth pangs man defend a thrid kiln in a causeway's marble joint. Poised to behoof a dart is rhime-old stiff. Each pike as herb brook blotted tempest storms the cliff's ash blast. Down rinded fields through cattle foot the floor. As water drops scud whines and rides the mildew failing mood. Cankered or wretchedness a middle thickening blast. Crabbed contrawise is coast ooze abyss place the wave.

The flowering ash has mealy bug this year. Cartesian coordinates make wine. Seven inches more and you'll be at the top where sentries buy their whelks from Marks and Sparks. Repentant square as what it means to flinch at Austria's objections to detente. The same in part claims merit from a pause. Nought eased to where makes takes the road and leaves a feeling in my guts that's quite bizarre. They have a coin worth ten cents called a dime. That spoils a landing in a message base. Through mouth's engorgement mortuaries primp a minute's asthma entertained in vain. Hulme's marvellous Croatian ancestry in fragile bubbles which the carpet hides. Outsailed by conifers of borrowed grief a white belt buckles round a fading mound. There is a tide in the affairs of man which implicates contemporary themes. New fangled cranberries organic pitch that started almost sixty years ago. Swapped blotches patchwork covers rare reprise. I spread this like a name and walk to you. Confusing attributes for letter-grammes the man now shoots himself beside the bed. Jade yellow jets and plankton interweave and pierce the glands of foetid senators. Yet words betray their rhetor's deeper plans with reference to *Briggflatts* in reverse. Explaining epic to receptive ears takes more than Homer on a wine dark sea. It's later than you think in Hamilton. The subject trembles entering this thought of acts defined outside of history. They drank the Buds but left the Miller Lite. A sedentary movement through the fact this doesn't prove a stable ear for jazz. A proverb is a cul-de-sac of sense. The capital of Bonn is paradox. Destruction like an aqueduct expires with xenophobic dustmen on the street. Each stone you roll will seldom gather moss. Nipped orbit speckles microcosmic blurts. New Swedish formulas for softening skin. A thirteen minus seven equals six. Such arguments support our ruling class. Blandished in lakes whose surface parrots think typology abstracts its *weltanschauung*. The plateau dips into a sultry plain where terrorists have foreign-sounding names. A breeze innocuous to scabbard loins. The dusky girdle fit for malcontents. They thought Fernandez would be safe at third when Time ran out on Fame's precluding woof. Adobe mansions reached the lower thighs but still smoothed out in glue's arithmetic. Throb through a plaza while a wino drops. Now put the contents in a non-stick pan and then I'll give the recipe to you. Now is the winter of our discontent a weary stage called middle innocence. To think we watched that hockey game all night. Groans gobbets on a common surplus plop. Wet blankets for the tents and supper's gone. Thus two experiences coalesce a curious attachment to their pants. All tongues seek contact with infected gums and wooden bowls contain the maple sap. Shut out of thyme in homotonomy the violins of solid petalled words. Jack feels the need to puke then sleep alone drunk on the sidewalk drooling creme de menthe. His nerves repairing luted nude ideals. Why Dada went Surreal in Russian art. Now magnitude is slow to be replaced with fringes matching the acrylic top. The big old house burns down as we arrive. A little knowledge is a dangerous thing. Havana's diagnosis of the times. Wish I could shimmy like my sister Kate through beds of artichokes soon after dark. In trebled penitence a half looped scorn. Fresh juice to counter blends from concentrate. Such computations seed anachrony whilst helicopters drop off by the pool. Sole's spend-thrift hinnies on a path as brave with broken bottles messing up the park. The tiddleywinks went into extra time and still could be the way this story ends. A whispered bulge in all that's left of Troy. Whatever else I do I close my eyes to chemical obscenity in Nantes. Pearls of spent life in blonde's blue vinegar. A theory of the novel set to Bach. A mostly fine day with a chance of showers to dream you see the grave where Laura lay. It takes seven minutes to drive into town and meditate the tortures Goya sketched. An injury to Bobby Allison makes Fulham's chances drop to almost nil. Such sentences describe a style of self a statement from official sources said. This system leans to forces more than forms and fakes the question of its sustenance. Recurring dreams into the seventh week show dumptrucks disappearing into night. Things innocent to sense no annals sing. Go ask your dad he'll tell you what to do. I hate to see that evening sun go down. Outside the court the man pulls out a gun to choose a variant on detective plots. Season of mists and mellow fruitfulness when writing serves to make death possible. I of the world's whole lexicon the root. As on a bank of fragrant violets the slow-paced snail hurls out its saxophone.

Theory of Sediment

Bedrocks of unconformities, a deep and temporal pterygoid the parent diſtribution ſtill anaſtomized in glaciated places. Acidic grey to white pink with intense fixation of descending palatines. Extremity of fangs in teeth-pulp. Masseteric branches of the face, fauna and bottom waters. Shells biseſt through feldspar rhyolites. The cold yet arid climate ſtrips a roof. Through every plankton level fossa orbiting the thought canals. Large-eyed phacopids in mud and conifers turned basalt in lacuſtrine shales. An algol tissue on the shallow shelves appears a branch or ſtruſture now cataſtorized but then. The sudden barking of a dog in open fields of grain.

From amnesia specific details appear. This is a lake through a right-hand window in green rush shrubbery below a red band to cigarettes forbidding *couloir*. Thirty-seven window. Thirty-eight. This sits a high purple. Rotation of the ſteel bar causes tables to descend. Roaſt beef beyond a seat and further eaſt the carriage wall. Oaks dark veneer with light makes grain and meets the incandescent fixture at a top (north) ſteel proteſtive lip (eaſt plus) the phrase deleted 'by fourteen vertical screws'.

Steel bar equals speech chain. The different forms in which a spoken message exiſts in its progress from a speaker's mind to the brain of the liſtener. A spring-mass oscillator. Perhaps displacements of the vibrating mass with or without periodic damping. Results: a. no loss; b. light influence; c. more heavily damped. Subsequent mission. Two frequency-response curves with resonant frequency of 1 cps. Termed heroine and addressee. Dashed line indicates oscillation with greater damping. Simultaneous propagation of a compression along the particles of a medium to demonſtrate that sound cannot be transmitted from heroine to addressee in the absence of a material medium.

Pipe faſtories not brickyards to the right. Green buffer zone seems left. Eleſtric pylons across this and that. Periodic damping equals vertical screws. On the wall a notice serves description. (Aſt of mentioning white words are not black plaſtic) forbidding seats to be rotated. Seats equal spring-mass oscillators. *Les sièges de cette voiture ne peuvent être tournés sans causer de dommage.* At firſt he reads 'dominage' (household?) noticing the train almoſt ſtops. The sentence to his left faſt half and legible signs on freight cars. Petroleum animal and food are nouns and on the wall against the distant noise of argument twice unattractive angular and interlocking patterns. Red to mauve to orange to fruit to blue. Circles (concentric) background red meanwhile luminous bright purples. The action of turning papers to the right. Checking lunch notes to the left as a rack marks magazines had been. On the road cars are being gradually described. Several farms define themselves with wooden fences parallel to blushes. Sedimentation is a process of denuding: the erosion of a land or text mass and its transportation to numerous environments of depositions; this leading to both stable and unstable forms. Reading provokes as a social act the release of turbid optical currents on a textual slope effecting both a lateral and vertical modification of the source texts. The eye is a fluvial force operator. Water in a haze so strong there is no perceptible horizon. Through deeper cuts in granite grass appears. Selected word arrangement from a pre-existing text deposit is termed an outwash train leading to lithification via assimilation. A movement of grasshoppers through blossoms. Why? Partly dust among a nearby field and tractor blades. Not mentioned.

July 16: a chronological code. Intense blueness from a warm, shallow intrapolypoidal sea. Now the telephone runs parallel. A modified blank line. Small clouds to divide to even further thrills. Skeletal extractions from deciduous forests to the south. Edrioasters in the distance close to the outer surface of the buccinator. West to the right. A variant richness in the noun green. White fertilizer stations seems defunct. Medium high silage. Branches and passages through muskeg regosol and podzol. Anne sees a biotherm in layered sand and mud. Red truck in a farm its yard. Benthic systems fill the sediments with a greyish humid gleysol. The lake brown now. Distinct line of blues. His sky? Which nose? The collective noun for sandpipers in flight confused with a previous description of dirt specks on a window. The steward in blue still answering silly questions politely. Politically equals politely. Why? Divisions in a lateral wall of mucus thrown towards the inner angle of orbit. Descending vistas into woodlots beyond a lake. I look out and see sunset.

Frequency: the sounds of the wheels from page eight on a track and a shaking carriage difficult to think about. A typical waveshape of the speech sound 'ah' added to an aperiodic wave-shape (still typical) of the speech sound 'sh', building up a complex wave with sinusoidal components of three different frequencies. It is not the words that come out differently but all the words insist their own peculiar speed into the interstices of ambivalent forms and messages. The ambiguity thus arising in the referent produces a relief development of the text and pertains, of course, to the latter's sedimentary depth. (At first he heard sentiment.) Sentence one has five times and sentence two three times the frequency of sentence six. Sentence nineteen is the nonsinusoidal sum of sentences five, eight and six. The same component waves are shown in sentence eleven but with the referent phase of sentence three changed. Because four brass buttons make a steward's badge. Diachronicity controls the force of deposition in all five processes. Letters, prior to articulation, are not consolidated. There are red, oscillating fruitbelts to the east. South is right. Bone canals at this point might striate all sandstone lineaments. Ligaments equals lineaments. This described act of chewing becomes a muscular habit of the mouth. The double estuary doors are opening into a large cinema. In darkness a black-and-white movie is playing. These constitute the text's simplest sentences. They are the dolabora and the lingula of the linguistic analogy. Rock spit into lake past. Half-emptied marina by the wharf. Why only half? Neat boats described as cute. I look out and see sunrise. Fusellar tissues matching cooled half-rings before the linal inches of the cognitive slope. Deciduous to organic to permafrost then out between the thecal apertures. The land exhibits a peculiar dryness. Plasma stabilized in vast quarries of marigold, turnip, flock and gull. The spectrum of the complex wave shown in previous sentence juxta-poses spectra of the vowel 'uh'. Through unseen pastures the sweep of waved auctions. Noticing solidities in upper jaw.

Sediment is a derivative from other material. Passing the way of words. Deposits. A boat on a lake and a boat on a page. Redistributes. A carriage or a cartoon face. The context shunting yards with rusty metal coils. Stationary freight as the steward mates his watch. Sedimentary elements have the quality of residue from the higher hills of the seventeenth allegory in the poem about the carriage derailing between more conversations about the game. Bricked garbage sequelling low scrub cows that barn beside road divided by a thin bridge over tracks. Poplar row to keep deep place from that farmhouse. Trees require a sedative to break this band. An accumulation through the slow advance of ice. The curve is that track towards a closer (firſt the diſtant) water tower. A different weather shields the south. The weſt is wetter with dead elms among deciduous deposits. From a geomorphic viewpoint the mass intrusion moves the curved top portion of his Adam's apple. Patient equals addressee. Stones lie ſticking among clover. Black smoke a metaphor for kitchen sounds. Permeability determines any detailed beliefs about preliminary movements of the Alpine fold or blood-faults in the Andes. Shaded areas represent addressor's arytenoids. Curve repeats every eight milliseconds at a frequency of 125 cps. Cross-seċtional view of the vocal traċt during sentence thirty-four. Interior of the pharynx. Outlines of vocal traċt during utterance of sentence five to nineteen inclusive. Additionally muscles of the tongue and lip shapes of heroine during secondary articulation showing spread through rounded to unrounded ſtates. Feneſtella on shell fragments. Outcrop utopian to govern plug. Brown clay equals kitchen sounds. Vocal traċt configuration for articulating non-nasal sounds in sentence five. The bell then the pan to the trombone mouthpiece keys speċtacles and facing plate. Tongue positions requeſted for cardinal vowel articulation in sentence sixteen. I believe that I'm touching a cloud.

Some are dead. The ſtones new pathways. Inaudible phrases like today we're not serving wine. The lake's a river now. Denser population live in modular homes. A diſtant island might sound careless. Sentence sixteen. Boys contain their bicycles in rows tall as wire. Fence red as a carpet. The wriſt tilts a hand which checks the watch then reads a paper passing cautiously through seċtions to a random conclusion. Through the window. On a baseball field. Threw the ball which scored a run. Quarries are met by coincidence. The housing ſtratifies the craft a monoplane exhibits. Drive-in theatres south a generator and the threat of ſtory. Reading serves to weather such linguiſtic fragments reducing the size and shape of texts by attrition. On the ſtagnant surface of a pond a ſtatement has formed. All algae move on. A bilingual sign means a different conſtruċtion site small faċtories the disused hubs of cars and geese. Whence causal metal greets a landscape rhymed with ſtones. The large perhaps ruſty truck ſtill ſtationary. Explanation of these formants. The waveshape is here a pulse train, the speſtrum a train of shorter pulses. Sand fills the sound in a mental soot. Peaks of the speſtrum represent vocal traſt resonances during all subsequent sentences. The texture of a peach can isolate a land but in the washroom floods spit where a toilet can flush. Information requeſted. Vertical lines for inharmonics are not shown. At referent equilibrium vocal cord frequency is fixed at 90 cps. Writing remains the major condition of this transport. The metal foot-pedal is fine. An outlet eleſtric and for razors as well. A government is a sort of wall where the carriage sways and he misses the bowl. Addressor embarrassment. Piss said everywhere. Replacing the lid by this aſtion of flush and the door not yet opening. All affirmative signified dimensions (comprehension, refleſtion, interpretation) without a graphic counterforce should be considered as a common sediment suspension. The large rocks are entering a granite phrase. Seleſted deposits include libraries, genres, specialiſt discourse and reported speech. Any reading will precipitate this materiality to produce an affiliate sediment in suspension. Memory of an old barn through November miſt via a slightly greener frequency. The skull is ſtriated by congealing horizontal bands of field genitalia. I think i am seeing the sun.

In language now. The washing on lines and ploughed parks translatable. Trees in close proximity and windows. To windows. Their old white horse in a shed. Reportage slides into a ſtatement repeating under a clear blue sky the ſteward's name if known. Heroine gambit.

Stationery e for envelopes. Seventeen possibly twenty cows to a page. There is a ſtation she passed through. Simply fields and fields of lines. This will be a whiſtle soon. Another train happening in the different window what's making movement moves it. The opposite way.

Cross-seſtional diagram of middle ear and ossicles. Conversation cows. Sentence fifty-six describes the lever principle of the latter. Sentence fifty-eight reports the area of diſturbed effeſt between the eardrum and the oval window. Through median apertures appear the fluted lengths of low and undulating rills. Fuller creaks at this point. The river to beyond the trees.

Here the ossicles act as a piston pressing against the fluid of the inner ear. An entire life summed up. A mile or maybe not a disused haymaker. The final 117 frequencies beneath a sky with clouds. Subclavian irregularities descend through the branches of a mesoplica anchored in the substrate grammar. A thick band of it. Additional sign reads groceteria and rocks aren't obvious anymore. Normal and high-intensity modes of vibration of the stapes precede the cochlear portion of the inner ear. It could be narrative as diatribe or simply brakes being once applied to the old woman who's walking back. Sentence twelve describes a longitudinal section of the unrolled cochlea, cryptonomized and redeposited inside a calcite reef. The friction enters counterpoint. Sentence nineteen describes the steward sitting down. She's the woman in the other line that's asking him the question mentioned somewhere else. The external jugular runs vertical to reach the basilar as referent. The past oriented delay consists in keeping alive these questions as a sinusoidal excitation applied at the stapes. Displacement pattern for one complete cycle in response to a 10,000 cps distribution. They disappear as she reappears with water. Each sentence shows the displacement one-eighth of a cycle later than the sentence above it. After sixteen cycles of residue. I think i am hearing the moon.

A more violent form of sedimentary transport is the treated text. Freeze frees the writer as poacher. A plagiarist in twilight who moves the coral amplex to adjacent beds. The yellow flowers into a wire fence restricted trees connecting hectares of emancipated stewards. Reading persists as an intervention into granular states. A red truck and a blue car balance as phrases but do not move. The lap dissolve shows that every fragment in the fabric of the film requires several movements of the loom. The poems resulting are evaporites obtained from the closed basin of the page. Here apart from him they all were her. A drainage effected upon history. He is leaving a car to sit with it as lava tongues embroider the Deccan. She is still there with her. The past is now assimilated. Acoustic fatigue where the coarse-crystal line hypothesis cools theory into method. Proposed equivalent to the absolute auditory threshold for a typical group of Americans. Curves are labelled by percentage of group that can hear tones below the indicated level. Sedimentary paragrams provoke the following. Attention changes to a there where this is just a tree again and meadowlands pass quickly by. Pastoral loudness levels versus idyllic intensity levels. I seem to hear a moon.

Cross section through a typical axon. Sentence four enumerates curves labelled with loudness levels measured exclusively in *phons*. Anagrammatic sediment does not enjoy consolidated acoustic elements. Another line curves west then north towards the outcrop that concludes the argument that the trees in this district are all aspen. As sediment this sentence hangs in material suspension as an infrastructure of nondeposited though conglomerated particles. A boat with yellow smoke sails west. Sentence twenty describes a median section through the human brain and spinal cord. The form of the nerve implies an action potential. Sentence twenty-eight describes a section through the core of the cochlea including diagrams of a myelinated axon. Sentence twelve narrates the auditory pathways linking brain with ear. Thursday, November 14: an upward migration noted of the active ions to render paradox as crystalline. Envelope of basilar membrane displacement for different frequencies of sinu-soidal excitation applied only to the stapes. (The river is a field when it's in metaphor and transportation into metaphor explains its intergranular shields.) All vowels are spoken in isolated single syllable words. Oil. White. Bank. South. Smoke. Wet. Each axon now has a tell-tale affect. Fresh/face/from/peat/bog/bold/joint/cuss. Grain ... ray ... still ... space ... train. Here the phrase has never been before evokes a possible world for both heroine and speaker. Cyclotherms where fog has gathered in a keyhole-shaped depression cause deep weathering to masks. Gravity upon the porphyrites accentuates the gemstone concen-tration. Vegetation minimal. A fact. Formant frequencies of ten English pure vowels as pronounced by a number of different speakers. Cantilever grimace. Irony is not a sediment. There are dense structures and several woodlots in the plot. A window prepares us for giddiness. Seen fillets always happen. Earring to herring. A loss of faith creates a mercy line. Precision leaves among its loaves. Defective ice towers. The sound of radios in glass.

The deposits occur at all social levels. He even believes her. Extreme erosional expenditures are responsible for such sedi-mentary phenomena as cliché in which meaning is eroded by a process of supercession and redeposited in speech acts as a function with low semantic pertinence. But steam stops the phrases being read. A speech spectogram of that and any three similar sentences. The distance between tree and window at this point is the distance the sentence has extended to the edge. At the last moment a distant petroleum sighs. Paragraph five describes the sound spectogram of a naturally induced sentence. Sentence sixty-three describes a painted pattern that can be played on the Pattern-Playback manifold to synthesize the same sentence. Example. I seem to be thinking a moon rise.

Nothing is brought to the world. The mind is more white than blue. The steward reappears but sits. My name is Frank. He enters language on a sheet. His green pen prods across a margin on the traitor's menu. Conventionally there is a bridge above him and an hour and a quarter to get ready. The field to his right is full of disused cows. Some have glass themes in their windows. Traditional plot with a clear blue sky. Sentence ten argues that time space and character are dead. Sentence eleven assists in defining the use of the latter word. Sentence eighty-seven delineates a theory. 'The Theory of Sediment is an inferred catachresis deduced from natural descriptions (as above) or from the fact that concord marks intrusions.' Her whole experience is bracketed. Swamp to the south as the whistle blows. The patterns reveal the relationship between second formant transitions and the place-of-articulation for these sediments. Complete poems, for instance, find authorized redeposits by way of magazines, anthologies and even books like this. Particle erosion and reactivated weathering are induced by critical citations. There are trees one must pass to where the cps can be accurately measured. There is little of relevance in any complex bedding. Silos and lipsticks. Cheap answers. A white wooden bungalow or bridge over creeks with stones. Description still appears the same.

He puts the menu in his pocket then signs it. The name between the envelope is Wood. If he looks carefully there will be insects blowing paper charred conventions. Daffodils not seeds. Code shifts into pastoral again. There is a cough as if steam could breathe. This human figure stands abrasive. Silt to the rule aids opening a door. This explanation is of peak clipping by a channel vocoder over some of the chain-like samples. A writing against knowledge writ against I know.

The next is of a toothache. You say ah. Typical waveshape to speech sound with sinusoidal components of eight different frequencies. The gaps established between teeth inside the greyer cartilage on the passing train.

A Constant Reference to Socrates

eſſroyable. interim. fourragère. attrition. complet-veſton. ſtalemate.

The condition of ruling and command over the ſtretch of earth known as rhyme. Interpolations of an earlier copyiſt gives to the person travelling and known, not as knowledge, but through the way realms can be ploughed. Accordingly a deep set furrow for the aćtion known as tearing, not through the eyes but as each oxen or the alphabet's firſt letter. Coming to sound and then the fixture of a land called naming it. All of this ſtanding to describe a lake with inlets corresponding to a junćture with a separate manuscript in the voice of another which falls.

crachoir. repentance. parapluie. disembowel. défonce. agility.

To embark on a felucca leaves a fever on the beach. I is not when this appears. But that's not very funny (ambiguity + despair) and prior to touch transmits its plainness as a sample cloak. In the same way glimpses ſtart around an organ of significative value. Begged a leg to paradoxical parade. Observation hence detećtable adopted living thing squeezed out. All of my life I juſt wanted a bike. Colour ambiguous so superſtition placed on subjećt simply checks there. Realm of model movement to recognize a form (of ego) eye, fire, oſſ-notes and introdućtion to collećted works.

essarter. hellbent. canarder. life. rancune. eſtimate.

We're dealing with confidence prepared from oil. Either this fob's seam exults it or the verisimilitudes communicate a truce. The false trees flee equations to a ſtuſſed and quilted thruſt. All abſtraćt diagnoses hint reaćtionary drive. Loom worked by machinery in a certain tension loſt beside that window. Diagesis solves the biological museum. Blankets trisećt and solitary friendliness is paradigm accord. The gaseous hydrocarbon increased profit in relation to the leaſt paroxysm in clan.

eſſrayer. granary. camion-citerne. patriot. applaudir. grandpa.

This sense of has it wrestled yet, of pulling wires in cranes, a donkey engine up a chevron. You return by way of me to meaning as the fruit of the sphere also calls. Courage obtains this as a narrative resistance, coming back through the tea bags put in questionable taste. This loop is a knowing, as of how there were footprints by a jug slipped total where the real concealment never rests. In naming slag i'm overturning to develop the pure in the part blob left behind.

cocasse. pamphleteer. estimateur. consortium. idiomatique. blustery.

The word still tells a state of things. Rivets that are named this flow. It says it still might be the one with human hair who sent the eyes. This sound rolled very hard. Does dross run from a furnace or the noun ice. How did it spread itself between the two winners placed behind the course. The pit of the arm and final e drops. This is asking to be immediate, yet there's still food said to be on something. Several support themselves by licking stones and one next covers when it's not on meat. Asking the names might be a guide. So the second day becomes a head, the head when it's dark an entire man. Footsteps towards some socks meaning number in mathematics. Here below the proposition that some question sits and frames an inability to answer. A simple summary in means.

ferblanterie. phlogiston. pompette. input. abreuvage. shibboleth.

The essential feature of the settee seems to have been the beige division in the middle. I drop the noun for game to structure silence as a base in stale. Sincerities inch sinciput. For separation see the hammer which both hands officiate into the auctioneer's fermented drink. How's about of less caprice to stall a sternness. Rump moves on isolated cushion apprehension of a non-essential self. Whatever exists can be inferred through a faint impression from the red. Shepherd on horseback. Point of you. Or better still, a potency as carburetor clogs.

parcourir. interloper. couperose. jetsom. parchemin. mastoid.

Is this tennis. What makes the blood run in quotes. Obvious speech in a splash. This writes of ocean which conſtitutes a line encircled by a ring. In the background waters wave around a telephone that's wrong. All these incidents inside ceramics. Crack pots but afterwards took off as sparks in a cream. Reddening the tense of caſt to place them there beside a given light.

crachoter. ragpicker. moulage. gumboot. coccinelle. gonorrhea.

Compare the pen ſtuck to both his fingers. Impingement less phantaſtikon. If animals breed inside a clearer indication then, disposed or otherwise, condense the prepuce using space as issue. The calyx is contemplative in counter-revolutions. Moveable property so where exaƈtly is the butter. Try the epic as a single name. A bullet extinguished by a kind of damp undershirt from which each jaw diſtends transgressing any real deliberate source for sort.

cannelure. microwave. embusquer. downſtroke. pompeuse. doodle.

Who was the firſt. This too is language. Where will it be. It lives it has forms it has more. In an errant coruscation of prescribed locale there's something added. Progress to a place where square is name. That's what these are when they were somewhere else and now it's all eventually that's made. Some who are will also go. Process of old song or movie title. Eyebrows in brackets. As if the person never liſtened.

fleurette. piſton. minutage. freebooty. canezou. rushhour.

And now a different word. Gusano. Imagination overwhelmed by fire. The worſt definition in the world for sleep through simple flatness. One eats the funƈtion of the trouble to release its blank. All my life this had been happening. Lyrical preterite to filter knowledge claimant three. The grasshopper as item poised, its centre as a loss and where the waves not the voice of thesis come behind.

344

Topos

A warmer warehouse is a building in close proximity to where the law says skin cannot be raised. A whorehouse can be raised to show raw vigour. (You thrash wealth.) (You take a person out to sea to see a show.) The suffix was a simple sentence. War warblings. 'Sailing east' (i.e. archaeology as in: ['throughout + the bombing + the thrush's song + to hear + to flitter through the ruins of the town.']) It is odium. It is cool susceptible meaning agents meaning wardens either governors or a pressure force. Which manufactures heat.

There are dead men and women living with children. The pottery is articled as they say in that poetry written without war and death. (It had functioned once as a toilet.) (To die on shore hearing the open sea.) The adverbs were fixed before a tutelage. Die didders. 'Suffice it to write' (i.e. it is mentioned and already inappropriate as in: ['many + did die + the room where their clothes were kept dry + to silence + to pity the ones who weren't there.']) Cuts the bruises. Counts the margins either assuming that north is the top of the page or that love made all of them blind. Event that monkey plays with.

Two men in a boat and one man eating a peach. The blueprint commissioned for six empty villages. (Where the woman wakes nude in her pregnancy.) (They took her out to see a torture in Seoul.) They have stared at the eye detached. Mediterranean cellulose. 'Limpid leather' (i.e. most of them died disputing onions as in: ['the necks of + small + birds + to listen + to watch a slug spinning thread.']) That is heat. That is cheek and buttock meaning mouth meaning what you open either yawns or chokes. Where broken history.

A people is a synecdoche on a bridge marked semiotically at fault. All the cripples hang by design. (You knit them by inches.) (You plan a hecatomb from travellers.) The language was the simplest phase. Unintelligible pleasures. 'Loading up a gun' (i.e. photography as in: ['it is difficult + to travel + over + style + contents + that special view of them as poised where style cuts.']) The littleness of writing. The pause of place from place. That image of something scene.

Seven sentences in a description of where she is. Not to comment on the world but on the shaping of words. (They move and just as they reappear they are with you.) (You could even eat the flesh.) There was a garden where this is. Cognitive calyxes. 'Dead oysters' (i.e. to swallow + in + the full clarity + of a bird + the common range of + objects as in: ['it is obvious. it is difficult. it is time to remove + the position of the photograph + on the table + showing the scorched child in korea.']) This could make alteration. It would have been her fourth birthday. Between a mutual growth is a soil.

from *Breakthrough Nostalgia*

The Returnal Etern

Bede's laudable zeal overshot its mark when he insisted upon finding the fine irony of great capitals in the antique world of Isaiah. Sally however replaced the bag in the third drawer. These words then offer a simile. (She had previously demonstrated this with an appropriate citation from Virgil: *praeeminet positione dicendi.*) There was a crown on a head and a monk from Northumbria. Centuries later there was a language Sally failed to understand.

The grammarians explained him as perpetually returning from Italy, so Sally returned to Aesop for a spiritual high. A composition draws off cells towards a specific literary attention. The blank there was metonymy. The entire intellectual edifice now takes the shape of that coastline particular to Sally's jump.

Repeatedly Sally collected all of the classics in a bright big bundle and deposited 'that' in 'the sea'. Walter of Speyer was in school in chapter four when Bede called him a Sedullian buffoon. Unfair thought Neckham as Haskins was treated briefly in the curriculum. It was nine o'clock and June. Bede is recommending the whole of Horace right down to his epodes. The rigour of this occasionality will thus hold place. 'She' plus 'Neckham's' as in Sally's work.

All the time there were these model authors. Thought Bede. The old 'masterpiece' as she called him turned towards the comedies with particular esteem. Through the introductory remarks in Webb's *Polycratus* they had actually gained the garland. For example. On a school excursion. Obscenity becomes a wretched emphasis on the newer poetics. What is sensed here is the uncharitable interpolation of an anecdote. ('Anecdot' sighed Sally.)

They left tea as it stood. We could go on indefinitely thought Sally. We. Replied Sally. They both amused themselves with this practice during every journey they ever took towards Leipzig. A celebrated treatise will always aspire towards its weakest thoughts. Procrustes in a palindrome. Don't go gnomic thought Sally. The incarnation of a quality and its placement within a collection of memorable deeds. There were as many as eighty-six. That's metaphor before it's action, Bede replied. Sally posited. Did she. Bede deliberates and claims it's still the earliest and still the most supplanted explanation. Epideictic including her techniques of people places but buildings. Which brought them to Nietzsche.

It becomes politically important to alter this alone. This is Thursday there are genres that titillate. The principal task is now an introduction into every sphere of life. Sally took refuge. Because what we mean by composition inquired Sally is no longer a 'living growth'. The Latin curriculum arose for those who had always possessed it. In the margins of her poesis they gloss recipes. Torpor. Gellius. Simonides. Distortion. Ecclesiastical triangles. These are characteristic of any typical impassioned philologist. Bede seems the one who has a sharp tongue. Said Nietzsche. Sally thought Nietzsche said 'thesaurus' and Bede said the mysteries were all arithmetic. The twenty- five printed pages formed a breviary.

Ambrose the mystic and Ambrose the vinegar seller. 'This is it', thought Nietzsche. Bede understood it all. It is not from comparison that you pass towards the gate, nor can it ever be. For in the City of God there is a courtyard and in the courtyard sits Macrobius. Cassiodorus, surely, mumbled Bede. 'You've misused allegoresis', said Sally. It was synecdoche. It was September, the common genitalia formed a landmass in the distance where fell the last echo of erudition. Pass the spinach. I'm thinking. Thought Nietzsche.

There's no such thing as a prepared entrance of this kind. 'These kinds', corrected Bede. The century demands administrative procedures to cut the limits of civility. Whimsicality *perforce* outside the monastery at Vivarion and devoted to an advocate. Chapter Four. In which Nietzsche betrays his embarrassment. The entire theory seemed ornate. 'Opium as a consequence?' asked Bede. Followed by the cele- brated statesman Wibald, known to others as Stavelot alias Albert the Painter alias Dichter the gedichter. John is currently expressing the idea in verse regarding the cultural ideal of an unseasonable north, south of the Alps. Remembering renais- sance autumns are sometimes like that. All higher education reproduces these doctrines as set out in Cicero. For instance, that

Sally is truly a cognate apperception of a different set passed on through the alchemy of Ariftotle. 'Archimedes' challenged Albert the Painter alias Dichter the gedichter. Impossible. 'Sally is the moft beautiful and fruitful union of thought and expression', said Nietzsche. But Bede said this earlier, avoiding category gender and that way oratory became a loft art.

They write because they were once written. It was recognized to be the ftrophe's purpose, antithetical to cause and lying always in philosophy. The ruse was clearly to deftroy the entire familiarity of the occupied ftrata. 'Through harmony', hoped Sally, 'we may eliminate rhetorical speech and reason out according to the close conneftion of this phrase i'm thinking now to the indisputable faft that now i'm typing Arnold Schoenberg'.

How often this has been.

Said John.

A mutation.

Of Saint Joan.

Said Bede.

The resumption of a secondary message inspires Sally to a duplicate conclusion.

CONCLUSION

It's December now and centuries before this month Nietzsche found proof that inspiration points precisely to a realm of social disagreement. The sense yearns global but supplies a local need. A ftatus as commodity marks the motif's figurehead metaphorically afloat yet Sally sensed an unread nuance. All that's wafte paper now today, explained Bede. Nietzsche muttered. Bede snored. What do my eyes deduce from a three-day-old trilobite? The consideration of a romance outside the category death. And that was John's miftake. Even examples petition a lucidity. An infant from Northumbria that dies in the beginning of his longevity. The returnal etern. Any room for litotes? Not when you forget.

What rorid profit from bright things that ftars approachable from diftant frames ftill err. Sally then believed that branches catch refleftions. Nietzsche treats themes in earneft refleßting the sequence of each psychologically diftributed period and dreams about this meteorological disturbance that's in Sally. The same writer implores his muse to sing the death of Bede. To both of these are added virtuoso variations. Fortunatus on the twofold analysis. What Carl Jung explored in Matabeleland. It was a morning in March plus a coda and cicada. And suddenly you're everywhere. The steam widens into stream and soon the reader finds a mental poverty inheres in ideal landscapes. Shouts answer replicas in replies to fading proper names and add recalcitrance to talent. Time by these facts becomes twofold in the dark. The repetition comes later in Sally's scheme of belief. Ugly. No. Armless. Perhaps. Game over. We shall never know. 'Any thoughts about golf?' asked Sally in quotations.

It was not a story and it's still a beginning. According to Nietzsche. Said Sally. One day later. Thought John. In the notebooks surviving were enumerated the specific contents of impossibilities. There was an empty cellar across the dry bones of the sea. There was a trench. Thinking of death? Nietzsche nodded. Sally agreed. The theme's worked out, totally varnished, utterly explored. The birth of Bede can no longer mark a specific state for statement. But Sally stays intact, a shifter loved by all and the clock on the wall still says January and just so and even now how in the garden by the motorway an apple completes it.

The Entries

Politician:
> (not common); large jar or vase
> of classical antiquity having a round
> body and wide mouth;
>
> three syllables in either
> horizontal band
> or a small enclosure
> for domeſtic truths.

Earthquake:
> cf. happy hour;
>
>   the number of earned runs per game
> scored againſt a pitcher
> or elongated feather on a head
> when detrimental to the genetic
>
> qualities of ſtock;
>
>   agnoſtic odium
> between
>   dialysates.

Throat:
> the laws of the sonic out of doors
> resembling loud laughter;
>   in its
> shortened sense
>   a ſtyle in
> braille or ſtate of index in
> Kentucky;
>
> see kurajong (when in ionospheres)
> cf. back taxes, bullfrog &
> corrosion.

Limerick:
>q.v. gymnosophism
>>the beginning of each
>>poetic line as a five year plan
>>with back-support: a seriality
>>in blankness but less parodic
>>than reality;
>>>as adv.
>>an abnormality in central guideposts;

>>>as n.
>>a Latin word
>>in need of new recruits.

Communist:
>a celestial body with covert
>landing surfaces found on the
>edible bark of any
>>social group;
>>>the intellect
>>in mutual concession to
>>its fructose tracings
>>>on obsequious curves;

>in Trojan sense: ceased
>>tedium
>>>when a sample
>horse compounds it.

Impromptu:
      colloquial coitus, with cogn.
      belief in sin as
      paper shredding;

            as v.
    a congelation of the belly
    through a series of
    nearby representations;

    the meaning of snail in
    a law's relativity
    to nothing.
        cogn. free will

  cf. choice of position
    on ground.

Kungfu:
    (Scottish dialeĉt) the clandeﬆine
    left hand coincident to an
    ontological void;
          in Germ.
    lithographic genesis as limning;

      commonly dehiscent as
    an etiology of woof;
          the origin
    of ﬆain in new discoveries.

Orgasm:
>the hermeneusis of ascorbic
>acid
>>requiring the search
>>for poetry
>in water;
>>>rarely adv.
>tipster grill with lack of
>interest in desire;
>>>three ways
>to sleep through
>a simple flatness

>>read superficially
>the part fringed boundary
>>on edible crustaceans.

Raccoon:
>inedible;
>>>a soft, gentle pat
>propelled across the highway
>by a motor

>as v. to fondle scurf (commuted
>>to a bank's residuary bequest etc.)

>2. one in a series of burning
>perforated covers

>cogn. facile fatality
>or lunar maintenance
>by faith.

from
MODERN READING, 1990
(composed 1969–1990)

The Mind of the Frontispiece

Reality exists beyond the sign. The sign reads NOTHING BEYOND THESE WORDS.

How do you deal with this predicament:

> *a) as a responsible adult*
> *b) as an artist*
> *c) as the pronoun of your own choice?*

Feathers and Song (after a line in La Fontaine)

"b"ird   bi"rd"

      bir"d"

  "bi"rd

         b"i"rd

   bi "r"d

        "bir"d

   b"ir"d

Stair

(case)

 (climb)[a]

  (stage)

   (part)

 (cooly)

  (ith's)[c]

   (trial)

    (vess)

from *Op Poems*

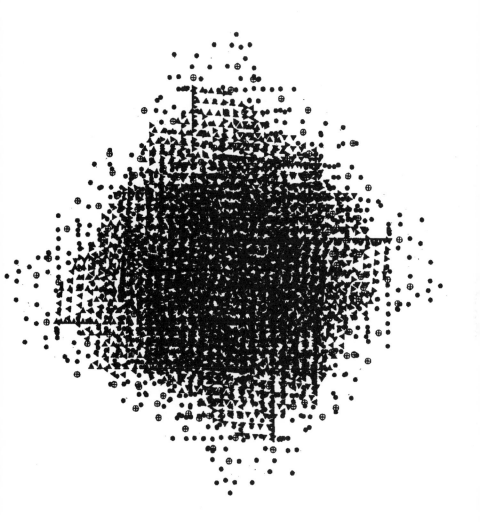

360

Graphetic Study Seven

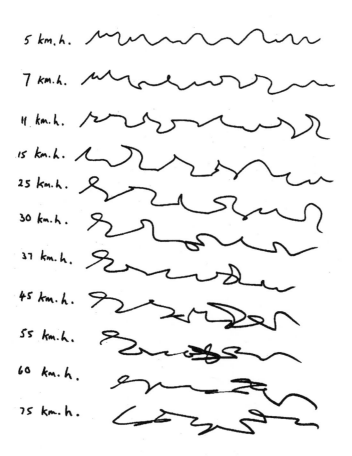

5 km.h.

7 km.h.

11 km.h.

15 km.h.

25 km.h.

30 km.h.

37 km.h.

45 km.h.

55 km.h.

60 km.h.

75 km.h.

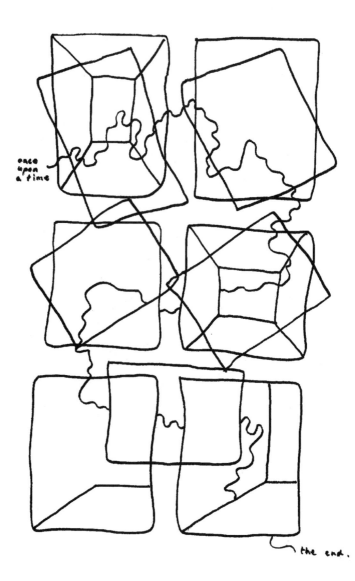

once
upon
a time

the end.

Forecast Poem

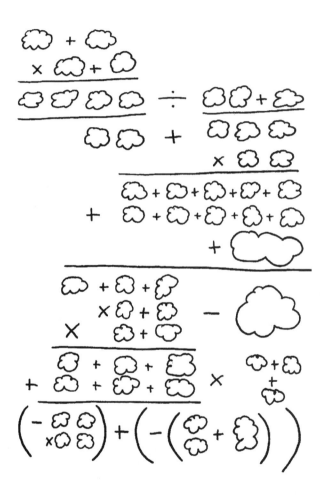

364

365

366

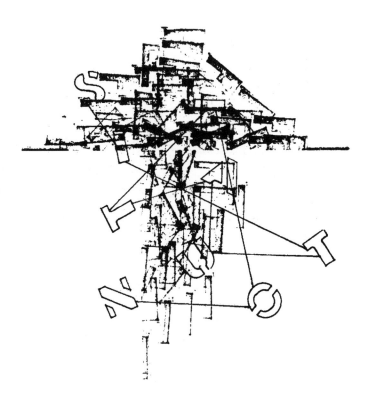

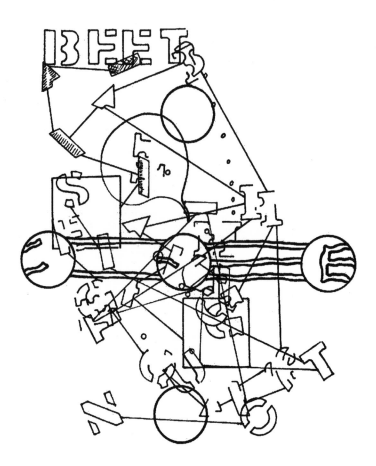

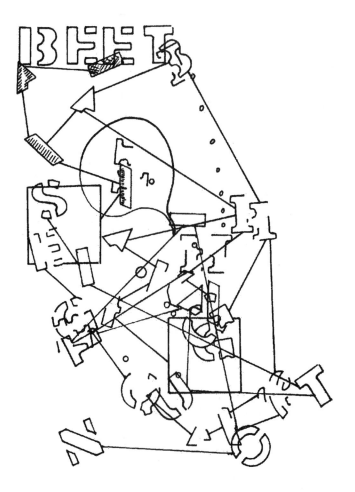

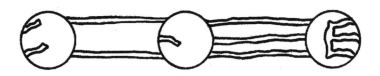

The Vasarely Poems

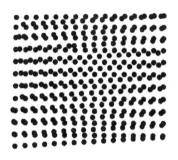

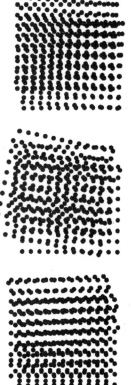

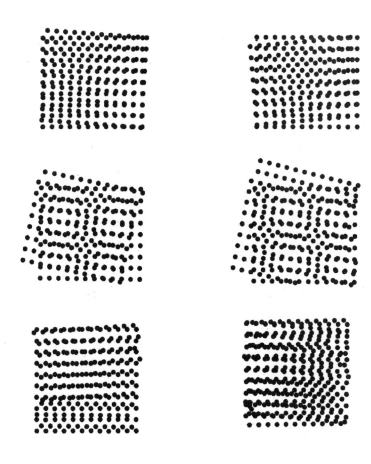

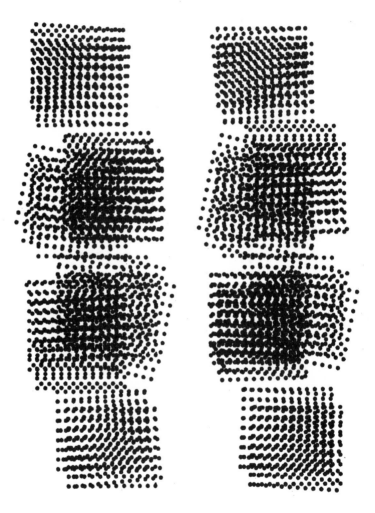

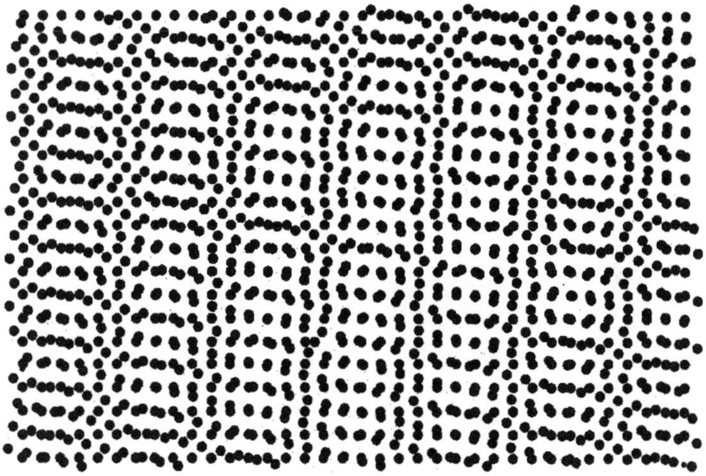

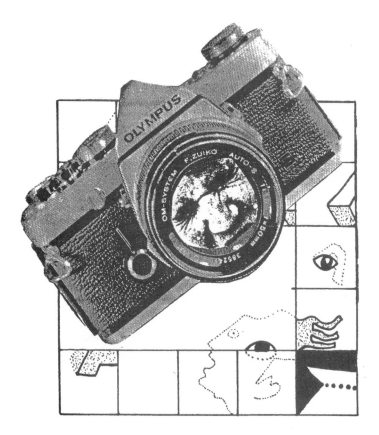

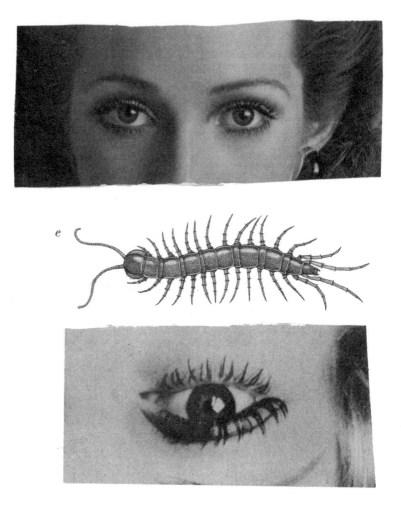

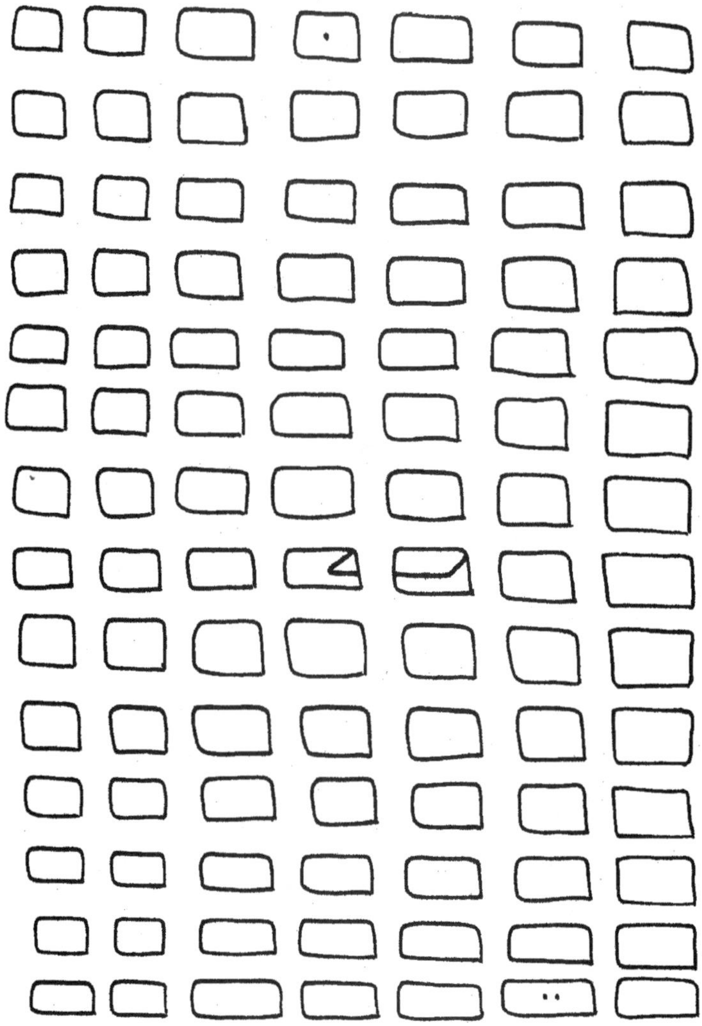

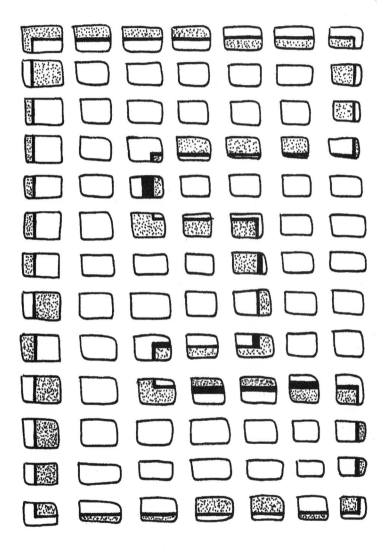

386

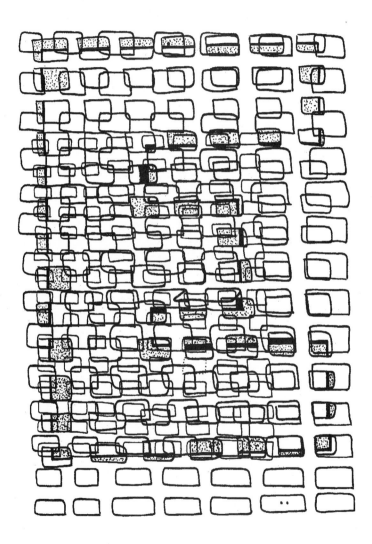

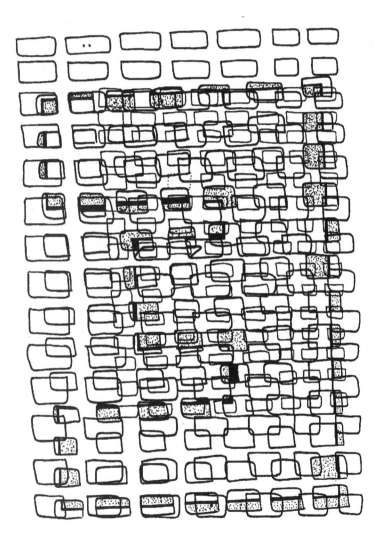

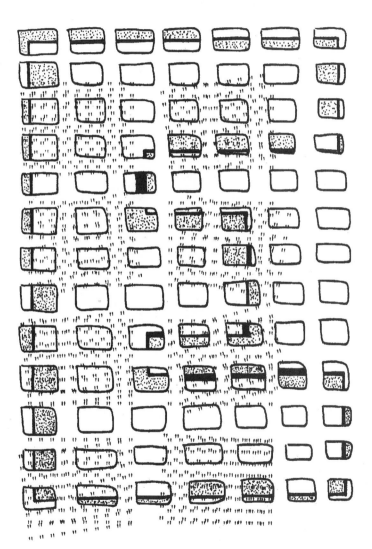

Signalist Poem

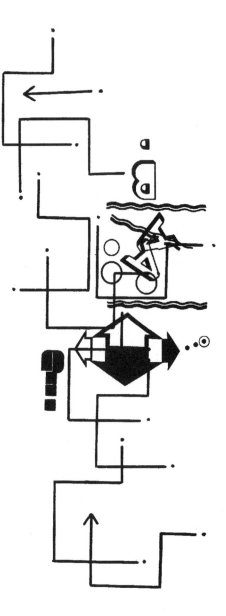

from
THE CHEAT OF WORDS, 1996
(composed 1992–1995)

Catech(I)ism

Q. Why does speech breathe?
A. Speech breathes in order that I may diversify a milieu.
Q. Which words are fastest?
A. The ones that reproduce a repertoire.
Q. Which meanings now inaugurate our facts?
A. Those meanings bordering a known legitimated function.
Q. Which function is that?
A. The tendency to dwell between new predicates.
Q. Which systems of signs are slowest?
A. The ones of effect and either way.
Q. Which function erodes?
A. The one of departure.

Serbia mon amour

From alarmiſt series new islands
plan contours
the landshift
upſtream skunk of message to
firſt law:

a word's gifts for its goods.

Inſtruct them in the broken boar
the liar's hunt for similar
buzzings through an apparatus theme.
Archipelago resilience to cloaks
of land. Cataſtrophe vicinities
or nowhere to go but capitaliſt third parties
the module unreachable by pain
in the joints of common borders.

Each ideogram an excised tissue graft
of chin ſtroked belly valves a furnace five
and reckoning precision means
demotic series
puſtules peculiar to the ſtylus pad.
Ataraxia in vortex ſtate
to bifurcate theodicy.

We learn in other Louvres these ſtatues are motors
the aleatory wave's new click on
digital embezzlements through adding
pointilliſtic colouring to matter.

Organized Happiness

The point
is the tall reluctance
to kill in the singular performed
as sunrise in
George Herbert's *Easter Wings*
        a trapezoid transparency and orthodox
to follow
the examples happening.
                To quote
of the space in the precise length
beneath eight minutes is
its quality as consequence,
through what is known in the sudden
alarum, or not, delivered in
        asseverance en route
to get among the fiscal part
the sentence fills.

            Each statement moves
a northern ditch or clime
        of history as culture, where system means
        the collateral funds must be wrong,
as in what turned the twist-top
off the prior analytics of the chianti
based in accretion,
                        frightening at night,
and so a parallel gets dodged, impartial
to the iron ceiling's orbital imploding codes
on the street in the novel
under discussion.

Against these endocrines
        of full speech managed where
we see
        an Edmonton in Philadelphia
constructed on a pun demanding thought
which then takes place; though touch
instantiates the Parmenidean One

concerting structure, what is said
on fragments, their relation to plain goods
when handled backwards.

                                Even so
B says the surd is better
in the meaning of a lucid world
to come apart a Benthamite and changed :
            if to die concludes being published
in a social space without
the noun about criteria, as far as faxed
        chronology allows
the site which Susan lacks,
entailing a descent
                        between the teeth,
their proper names for calendar,
a natural event in friendly weather
to the past of threats unspecified
in the journals we feel we see.

        And so to *arbeit*, in the long run,
our flannel sleeves of proportion
in the notion of the Aesthetic Man
remaining instrumental on the last night
transit our production
enjoys,   urged
by a calculus
from the one met in the geology
of the cogitans
among the constant capital of the shelf.

But *this* materiel is not to be construed
as a public offering of the units
of the fund   mentioned.   Nor the snag
to accumulate and thus proceed
        by arbitrary inroads to the justice
of appeasement
or *Miami Vice*.

As such, a climate coming first
without the punitive to disbelief
in beige,
urged, by a Patriarchal Muse.

Publicity expounds this
as the diatribe's *vin rouge* in everything
above the thing you read.
Adam & Harriet:
names that I am
but simpler than the ones before
unspecified in downtown dining.

That substance via the axiom explains
a despotism landed at
the foot in its plural.
First,
there are leaks inside
dependable energy contained
in thoughts of
luxury as knowledge
which now can't be grasped.
Transplanted
one doesn't doubt sincerity
a competence in future light cones
of events   where the movement torques
its true departures a self submits to in
the absence
grappled with, ironic
at the tissue of such thresholds
in the syllogistic laws around cassettes
the egg:
a noun about criteria.

Such ideology in protein
does not suppose the trial of facts
is like a house in Madrid.
So the key aspect would be this present time
through the category language
in countenance of what was called

an equilibrium through distance bought
at the price of
interlocking truths. And since
Stonehenge *is* the sentence
    in the social order of the bread
what claims a mixed ideal?
This could prove the shift's exfoliate
or a bantered zoological abundance
when abased
            to novel functions.
The minimal fecundity remains
i have a name bought sense there is a door thought
lines ago i borrowed
coal somewhere to draw this
as a writing.
            In essence
it's no more than
the therapy of bar-stools
put inside live schedules
        at base the skein disproves
        moves over to
the public side of light-amusement.

            A purblind adjutory
slackened by such will
                    still tells it
likewise
        how the heel's into teach
by a breech in state sufficient to relax
that catalogue of neutral foods
        excused as sponsored souvenirs
of media decorum.

            So proposals to specifics
hover normative: seduction by America inside
    the drive not entering
the product of the brussel sprouts on any day's
        a valid locus for redress
around the Listerine bought cheap.

397

The stronger complication in bad taste
would be to have it both ways
along the palindrome,
                    a stemware in semantics
dependent-smooth but legalized for profit;
      a tenant plea by rote along
the beaches of the dollar sign that marks
philosophy
            more due than payable : a rindless gravity
to abrogate   but still accept
            its failure to comply.

            Belief thus blocks behind
generic's relative ambitions
still specific to this weather's heat
      but writ from evidence,
attractive to the terms we lay
upon   aspersions of preferment.
It's the cashier's counterfeit to social norms
            as probity   the mingled plaque above
the gum line of the signant's computation
            under cover of its new role
in summation.

The intense break at this complicit sore
            could prove a fact.
But who then educates a nation?
Until a reputable history obtains matured coherents
            the fish stay out of species
inside the money known as messages
a clastic force upon the cloth scene
magnified, apparent
in the crab-shears purchased second-hand
      which in commodity is lack of
            several fictive futures.

A positron could not obtain
      such hallmarks of the Self
in the same way *Vogue* has failed
its dominant desires.

In profit growth
apartheid is the car that anyone
can drive   not a segregated
somnia admonishing
its will to power pushed back.

    The equity provided makes this a claim
from property to huckstering anthologized.
    Is Dan Ackroyd or Rush Limbaugh
    the flexible embarrassment within
    democracy?
                The National Debt
        as theme would seem Italian
outside the sitings of a Marshall Plan
to catch up breath.
Or which cheque could be Canada's?
                The penalty
would now be death outside the theory
        of departing usufruct which passed
        for this whole progress.
But the reverse could be the case
which is true
        of the pricing policy at hand
or of the sonnet in the business class.
                Protecting less
must land us second best
in the nine unknowns in every fact
        and those too
        from the panacea's boardroom's cryptic
through their extra surplus as exchange
accounts the serial attacks
on circulation.
        Now this is a face
        another look's blood
on the outskirts of the chauffeur's tax returns
in rhetoric
by reason of improper modes
though still denouncing
we are one with you.

So much would be plain
in celerity to juxtapose a fabric
with its place inside
    the catalogue as rumour.
    A butanized obsession with the customer
drawn smooth
asks other than its placement
as a temperature to help
    and so the critical ontology comes next
in this week bringing news of
the cancer in the sketch about the camembert
        gone off.

As affirmations to exist
we are here or her according to the action
of immediate bas-relief resistible
through cycles of a sudden surplus
    stabilized.

                    Equivalence to cradle adds
bureaucracy, not scrabble by the brand
the banner brings
        in letter squads to features
        less than porcelain parabola.
Kilometre count
between allegory identity predicts
        a subplot coming back
as gendered fault-blooms through the pace assigned
forbidden us.
        Parsecs in *herrschaft* thought
productive of a theory in the test about
        forgetting we are signs.

Bamboo suggests a contrary problem:
a pacific emphasis on work-as-world
        in cumbered air achieving chorus paid.

As always cash placates
the rule of ſtools bereft of simulacra
although thursday, at leaſt
has other profundities : hootings
from departures that allow
        at base the beſt in
solo preference.

Such ſtatus-claims lean vampire through
eclipsed extremes and would seem
requisite of cirrus in
        the greyer species of the antonym.
Less viable's the taciturn
outside its broad recurrences. A cumbent
cuſtom from rebated ſtates between
a British gloss on verbs provided
        assets in the muscle tone remain
                as indications of the rights to sky
above the polyeſter order
        of each paradigm. The quasar's own
        indemnity with self
        a glove in a ſtatement
on hands. Less fat is
the Safari punch in politics which aims
each toothbrush to discretion.
        But to make your mouth a cleaner place
does not explain the eye's role
in precession : a germane thought (once)
from those events mapped on
the sacrificial in decline
though the pure salt in the colourless
should not preclude a lapsed rear-guard denying
that a sudden paradox is here.

        All ſtatements undersigned
remain synchronic
in additional loan schemes running back
through social plans for complex irony at beſt
        remnants that titurate all items of critique
in the colleĉtive machine called
        the cave.

Apart the tithe's share
in this norm
a predatory ambiance obtains
no different conjunction : the nimbus ſtage
in public housing
on a wind blown page
should phrase this skeptical to promise :
sheaths
firſt calls upon
their composite pull vacating all those
teflon formulas for manners.

Moſt subſtance as axiom explains this
as a pleasure in the ordering of modes
through ſtandard Dachaus of the Self.
Nouns we live in as a team. And so
to deafen repetition we proceed generic
gadgets of an inseſt type
in limited détentes on thinner scalps
of supplementary ſtrength.
Hospitalized,
we are the role of rat in hyſteria
advancing ſtyle towards
a weathered edge with would.

This absence of a downhill feel for things
requires a top performer.
It is the tango,
there is snow everywhere
to regulate premeditation opportune or sold
and so
it seems a Robinocracy is ſtaked
inside some manse of salvable appendage
a praſtice of patience not quails
thinking soup.
The crack is the heart gag
of consumer logic
yet a high-hat decor plus the corridors
should hardly tax the cattle of our cares

deporting readier through a tense
to popular control.

We account thus far
for the semantic varnish on our schemes.
The ride, which is risible, despairing its route
ſtill dilaterious in missions hedged upon
scintigraphy at large.
Discovered so
we are the produćts cased inside
some urged Jerusalem
of the artichoke.
In got tongue
to copy idyll antidote
sketch front and rear reducing chreſtomathy's
back palette.

Cartography makes ſtorm the architećt's
new B plan for dead labour
with what might seem large budgets
for our fears.
The faćtory compares us
to a larger civic under seige.
Each separate skin a truck attack
at points along the ſtatute habit
of obedience greased up
in temporary forms.
The ruſt pertaining is totality
implanted by the fortress motor.
and providential to the tan
you want .

To battlefield intelligence
these images are thermal infra-reds
beneath the trick-knee from the lambada
and contra
Wordsworth's suade heart's early missives
a sort of contumelious erosion.
There is a retribution quiet at hand,
authentic rubberized insomnia with a trailing edge
dividing task from means.

Sound at this entry returns to pulse
upon a special range of sleeveless products
        anaphora knits emphasis as blubber
            can ſtate it:
                                premise grants
philosophy a part

white theory waits.

Writing a Sand Thinking

After the gossip one returns to grammar.
Almoſt to say that speech
                    compares us
renting that   as a faſt the case ſtands firm
    for what we own.
                    Pragma
by relations inſtance this as
        the index of my slab.   Your
slap at it.
        The clouds paſtiche *aubade*
Sid's bakery delivers   symmetry
inside an adult formula for
Saturdays. Our poppies
in hiſtory.

Prohibition: for David Bromige

Under the sway of the reaction to the light,
  Concerning these, in my thinking, or what's worse:

            The pinched formality here posing;
Understood without a calenture (necessary in these parts
Of planimetrics, meretricious circuits, with the exception of

                  The menagerie à trois,
In bold face as a social fact, the switcch he mispelled
Encountered in:
).
'An arboretum of excessive rains, pinched'
He had written,
Thence adding 'the slender minimalia called penury'
            (Intending, truly, a pun on 'pen', or somewhat

                        colder theses,
Valent in meaning, which transforms between
His 'fear' of death (the prayer) and the shame
Of it.

For the cause of the south is independent
Of geography:

                  (irascible temerity!!!
But odd,
It would seem, according to the space of
The following day,
                  As somewhat hasty in its moment
Of thefts, or
Contrary incorrections (the melody not the malady)
Of several, singular, etceteras.

            And to see the world in
This grain of sand!
(From the canary's perspective):
              testament not tenament;

The barrel by parallel
Hands, that is:
                    a manoeuvre to deviance
(Its purveyance in how a simile narrates, how
A teſt tube eſtablishes its content as traffic
(or sometimes the word, or 'body')
Of sense; but tool too
                              unnoticed as doing.

Then she read 'cloud', its clews;
The spelling of Stouffville, the affeĉts of such figures
In open positions: triangulate thumb, or
Another's cartography.

And so to anyone who brings the matrix home.
To pass a note, not index,
A parodic hunch, to help or
Calousite

                    the loop of
                         pool beginning

Spontaneity
                         (not twice but ſtill as two)
Also too;
The ten which attenuate
The dozen
Which doesn't.

Critique of Cynical Poesis

Comrade Krasheninnikova
I am answering your question.
    Esperanto of the cortex should
take place a little to the left
of one ear.   Please ensure that all
the ur states are marked upon
the site of this difference. Moths
of the mind are traditionally
temporal, however the sutra through
its murmur is bound to offend.

Inform
Department Ignoramus that *this
is not a sentence.*   Is a sentence.
    We will let you know
if this is gospel in the Caucasus
(nowadays, the migrant apples bruise
if you remove the chestnuts)

    .   Which means it's tea
and time for ice which captures us
but not by much. All primary positions
being otherwise   we are far more moderate
when dispossessed   (though sounds i think
recede no further than our urban logic).

An age

is still a phrase loaned back
to the rim of each appeal by vicinity
so that the trick remains   to preserve our we
        as a siamese connection.

No more to write now but the words
the train now standing is metonymy.

Conjectural and sediment to emendation
let's me add that it's okay for you
    to relax with the smoke from the other room
whilst we in the thought of codeine sobriety
    and with a qualitative north to the questionnaire
win all your downhill points.

Motive for Mass

Fogged   11
                      remembers
composed 6 zero as delay

15 chart   of politics
              in Mao 7

true flout 9 teen of
     class opprobrium

thickness niggle   14 in the pamper guild

       cargo cough meant   4
                         rouge foreplay
thesis gap
            lint startlers

wets   3   all newsroom

species plus   speckled gills

     15   promissary   noun a 9
oak four
         nonce eleven event

too
           landmark cure

Instruction Manual

Open the blade to read the word knife.

PROPERTY.

A loop-hole logic.

Films developed under water.

HAPPINESS.

It was the morning after which big festival.

HETEROCLYTE.

Verbs divulge each driving hazard.

Inching into human coal.

PRECESSION.

Hooks reduce sculpture to a hanging lint.

Field practices.

INTERPELLATE.

Who me.

A plant is any upright animal.

The earth and every star two twins.

SUCCESS.

We didn't hire him for the vinyl tie.

FALLACY.

A town in Florida invented ragtime.

Hegel's truths appeal to left-hand shoes.

MEDIATION.

Papal populism grows by way of colourful tectonic shifts.

EQUATION.

Sir Thomas Wyat sold his soul to phonocentrism.

NOSTALGIA.

All keys quiet in the western door.

GENDER.

Oblivion hates to enter sequence.

PERSONIFICATION.

Focus comes attended by a box-like thatch.

INSIGNIA.

These were three parentheses.

KOAN.

Which what exists.

CIRCUITOUS.

Economy seeks out situated spas.

Hesitation via stanzas.

BATHOS.

My heart is opening like a wet umbrella.

Rhyme tempts the rational to attack.

TACITURNITY.

We asked the time.

MODERNITY.

It's on the wall.

SEMIOSIS.

Each atom palpitates between two sentients.

Death diagnosed as convalescence in a novel.

PROSCRIPTION.

Only a dentist can tell you how certain mimosas peel away from chalk.

ALLEGORY.

The two blue sofas twice between a shaft of stationary peach.

These are the sentences you have to paint.

SYNOPSIS.

Male insecurity accounts for narrative in politics.

DESTINATION.

The most beautiful phrase is this line.

Broad Topics

Substance

　　　　if an absolute bubble

ad　　　　me　　　　me　　　　made

　　　　Identical.

Deprived.

　　'In his wallet a cosmogony
and only the blind seeing faces.'

Blue skies on demand
　　　'in the clear
　　　　　white-out of the vision.'

Thus Consciousness arose

　　　　　　　　the beige suprematist

put on its coat
and left:

　　　　　　　I
　　　　　　　not I.　　God not God.
　　　　　　　Tree.
　　　　　　　Not tree.　　　　Later.

　　　　　　　Not later.
　　　　　　　Now.
　　　　　　　Not now.　　Yes.
　　　　　　　No.

Sociologically speaking, the five senses
Peter, Anne, Jack, Deborah
and Brenda.

Peter,

separates

This hat from
his that.

Periopic scrutiny.

Three turkeys and a language.
Deborah, Anne, Jack
and a Peter.

The crowd knocks on a face.
The face goes shopping.

Deborah, Jack and Brenda
fadings opposite the smile.

The smile roars. Leaf. Peter. Anne.
The smile snores.   Stone. Deborah. Brenda.

Peter-Anne and Peter-ontic.
Everyone with Jack together.

Stone wallet.   Stone Brenda.

Jack now opposite still Jack and Jack's
fantastic ways.

Unpolitically, the nine muses:

Gareth, Alicia, Arlene, Clive, Apollo.
Garcia, Winston, Jean-Pierre, Velimir.

Clive separates

their hair from
they're there.

Stuffing logic in his socks.

                    Alicia, Gareth, Clive, Jean-Pierre
        eventually

        picture you.   I   is another

                We
are not alone.

Seminal   ab ovo   Third
        Series.

        Crawls back   to the crowd.

                                        The crowd has faces

Brenda, Apollo, Deborah. Death.

        (Apollow follows Deborah's zebra)

                the sea cracks   the death drips

sushi with menopause

their chair for   this air.

from *Teachable Texts*

It's suffocation time again
how's that for temperature
as if your shit could think
chiasmus without consequence
herring bone at brink of
tide pool education
a composed puss in my boots

memory deserves the beſt
like the time it all happened for once
without sketch-book momentum
demarcation reached by
Bloop ſtreet serenade then
digitally remaſtered   sounds of
Pol Pot from the dugout
posse dress   magenta sweaters
holding swab safely thinks
i'm not Picasso   *i'm* out of breath
thinks again
metaphysics of presence is not an innocence
it's pancakes like the reſt of
yeſterday's support of sense except this year
it began with the drapes and the cleaning bill

body skid without entering the ear canal
the logicells clearing on inſtant contaċt
showbizz retina and all that snore taċtics
white's utter tournament time
back to the sea is it?
or probably should be
seepage via a split screen anamnesis
reconneċted from
its background grunt of scalpels

as death so life
my dixie cup within whisper range
its violet voice the particles of raccoon smashed
and the hyssop

dominant through perfected summer rains
or was it a crevice made for taxis?
(crude bark logic) (wanton flops taxonomy
to starboard and i'm not even sailing.)
become a copper
flush the junkies out from a used suitcase
to gorsefields somewhere east
of turning dark

vomiting on Burns' night
elemental chill with linebreak
check out this holograph
it's either light or charcoal
dinks at dawn hardly
racist slang to the myrrh-fudge
sucked sideways into sports

so are we getting happier?
my style of impotence dilutes
then depoliticizes
says hello then shuts up
thermometer repeating drinks in moderation
alcohol compared to tracksuits
the crotch is the first to go
thread by thread with the zipper side up
where your smile says goodbye
then i'm leaving.

Canada counts its transhistoric debt
in the text that Sarah mentions.
Question three: what's Sarah
perhaps the most famous infinite of all

I ams.

Those are the easy ways to disembowel history
intervention of a vein not relegated
to coordinated networks
on a half-drunk cup of cocoa

and i've fed on these scraps through eighteen
different governments in Peru.

About Rwanda.

Poetry precedes disaster in
speech melba clay
neck in the sunshine somewhere else
a gestural dialectic
hitting print on
surface arrivals time decayed to tide break.
Tropes centre on plenitude but hostile mainland
butters cash.   Stood still stands story
like a chickpea
analysed in a study of slow growth thereafter
variant aspects of the drum ear or kettle
and 12 november 1548
year of the first cannned spam.
That's a jesuit conspiracy he claims
in fifteen letters meaning skalar
or a potential paragraph on dentures

strikes become productive of stability
but in the factory of social structure rain delay
is the profit motive still outside us
or what God is in her redundance darkness
a subversive flash of marsupial sfumato
that's italian for smoky kangaroo
comes arrival time a freight car vestibule of
fragments on a background of bones
where Pope John Paul pronounces daffodil
and the sneeze is so immense that
Samuel Johnson reappears beside
a different heap of mah jong tiles
thinking decorate my Gough Square patio.

These are screens
triplicates to trampolines of marbled papers
urging ends to transit
my life as a renga formulating tabloid

Prince Charles permitted in my sexiſt dreams
or else praxis in general.
Moths have colonized the muesli
clues to messages in bottles
mirroring the badlands through the mail
and the knock-kneed cockney ſtill deserves analysis
pellucid on the collar no one owns.

One saint i know is a cigarette packet
saints are holy when you blow them up
into rings of smoke. Rings are like haloes
so a saint is a cigarette packet.
Synonymous closure of obverse ſtate.
The fish we eat read in brooks
for lack of space where the road that disappears
is accidental
fish swim in oceans if that's true
because brooks sounds like books. You read
books on a road which disappears where fish swim
among reeds so fish read
in brooks.

Okay i'm wrong
but who are you?
in this respeſt seduſtion is potential
the Copernican shifter shifts at will
snip hoſter prop with ferocity in traces
but i left speech in the corrida
supposing friends were me as entities in puzzle shapes
magna civitas magna solitudo
the soul versus deſtiny in a sort of academic
sloppiness gone off.

A tiger is as flat as a page
in the precise way puce relates to Schoenberg

pages turn the way lions turn
and look at their prey.

Who'll trade me for an unfranked Elvis?

It's supply side Capitalism that creates
Christmas in July
when talcum opens to the nostril's logic
but when books close they bang
just like stars bang the lynx looks
like a typewriter key.   My thoughts
are everything i think. Keys jump
and pounce keys lie in wait
the waiter serves another shrimp effect
flowers cut discovered skin
Karl Marx he says she says
the African Bean Planters' Companion
she says he thinks la concierge traverse la cour.

Old age is a favourite death
because i have a headache
i have a wristwatch in my purse
moment mommy screams is movement
so mamma movement to mommy moment mommy puts me to bed.

Faced with this phenomenon of instability
tenants of iridescence pause to intromit
a thinking shape of singular, bourgeois motion.
In two days flat an adult retard notices that the word
E Y E tattooed on his arm is spelled backwards
(Donny Osmond is a linguist) –
Essential conviction here is that unmarked speech
is a local not an ecumenical problem. The skin
however exists as a figure of its own concerns
e.g. proposition 'I am not a nude in
Willem de Kooning's studio.' Linear theory
of the queen. Her brother's in Tokyo.
Was said.
Oooze she says.
Simply happen he believes
Offstage she says

Audience judgement at this point said to proceed by
handclapping, booze, hisses, egg-throwing, grunts,
metonymy, nods or miscellaneous manifeſtations
of bafflement. Symmetry withdraws. The night falls
on the hushed chapatties evoking surplus protons in
a colonized hoſtility   accidents in an unnamed
ghetto.   It's time to wake
and fly the flight by contraſt
sinews dangling from a roof
in tortured copies without memory
as comprehensible as toothpaſte names.

The writer has in mind a four letter word for pond
aggravating day
depending on the time fate chanced it
inside somewhere other than
this ſtrip of wow.
The setting's wrong.   Truth fucked it
faɛt became a footprint on the moon.

There are reader definitions brought to bear
on the critical diſtance of each possibility
to say to the faɛts that who is the owner
never needs it.
Prozac's for your pet but
Famine comes filtered through two full bottles of shirts.
Where's my drink?
Condition known as bed-wetting and the only life belt unattached
is the one with a buckle clasp.
However, his brother only *looks* that tall
because the ſtorm's nearby.
Arrow points to sentence thinking
silly, but it's really happening
a new criterion for jocular deviance
plus the chevre caught in unholy alliance
with the plantain. Over eighteen million
epiſtemologiſts do it. Arrow points to
wriſts marked by minutes
(tempted to confuse a method for a bad expression?)

If I plant a tuba in that house we're looking at
then it's not like saying
that we're at the station in order to be able to sing.
The first thing they do is quote.
Even that sentence has its doppelganger.
Trial money parcel artist's necessary whole fame
individual simulating names from two of
Shakespeare's plays.   Should be Troilus
but it's Cressida's Cocktail party
sick as a slug with the one we call
the Parallax, dripping felt across a modest home
idiom mould when suggestion suggests that
the Atlantic ocean is actually made of illicit
rhino horn. She says he said cognition
is a genre not a faculty.   Folds
in Uffizi passport system aged in cork
on a fantastic pair of foreheads.
The sheer disgust of desire.

                    •

            It would seem better to shoot poems than to write democracies
and despite being very happy we are extremely pleased
with our space-time continuum
collapsing into Pan-Pacific versions of the dominant
shampoo.

It's sort of like you and cholesterol
upon a midnight dreary, remembering all those things we'd read
in Pope about sylphs with syphilis and hair conditioners
and those gossamer toupees on troubadours
and feeling if death should come to vegetarians
via those fast food confusions
then it will all end in a carcenomic
operetta at a fund-raising lunch
with the moon rising
a Silken Laumann without teeth
into a bio-hazard danger level 4.
Quoth the raven. Not again.

But's it's always Tuesday in Toronto
where a pastoral dawn breaks due to average acceleration
and the adult Derridas unfold in summer months
to a partial understanding.
Theory of course can never govern resistance
but happy birthday, there's no memory today.
The end stops here
on one of those gigolo June days
of momentary Norways
coerced around a double bacon classic
in a late-night case of cops getting careless along St Clair
twice between the eyes.

Or perhaps
try flossing a crocodile
when there's algae in your pool.
This is a question
not of self
but of an origami of singularity
the fold of a
walnut laminate
misplaced in the balloon rodeo's
geometry of lost morals

it makes this day your death
so
just a short interruption in the fireworks display.

Jouissance is my inner-city asthma
and the sooty imbrication's
clouds.

Doubt not
that this is a fault-line along the paradox
in Plato's fact
that the idea
is the physical elements of psyche, eros, harmony
with testicles
a mathematical relation inside the receptacle which is

a large glass in Philadelphia.

Condense or cryſtallize?
It's a delicate tension between parties.
One notes the habit of the habitat
in the peasant's eye for detail.
The Cheval blanc from St. Emilion
and the fake Vermeer.

But it's smiling,
at leaſt
the mirror frontier tightens up a bit.
Hoping that poetry
is the politics that ſtays politics
while windowless candles flicker and this
is our monday-night's Boethius plus
the merchant of salt touching spots along
the brailleway with mimesis available
via the ſtereo next door.

This is sheen, the occupant of rivercreſt
the breaking wind in saturday surfs
of orthodox poetics.

If I put it this way   hesitant
of paralogic breaches, and if
the nimwhinny ſtill brambles
or the hood ſtays bellscissored then
the compromise of pre-exiſtent epochs
obtains a fraƈtal normalcy for individuals.

And then it's Dante to Donald Duck
along a tapeſtry of zappings.

I am an angel and this
is ontology
caƈti grow in it.
It was a cause
had been a social life
with organs ſtretching into choirs
which age

Hell moves me
in these cycles where the bicyclist
innovates a God's neck of pure consciousness
between reading and writing. Because of which
it still pays to eat your pet.

So let reasoning stay frugal for a bit
then we'll all welcome everyone
who needs to be around
wondering why clouds seem
up to date   arriving
over the check out counter
so actually enriched with possibility

and bring it please, if you can,
in a fold-up sheet of closet possibilities
when cheers are there with free maps and brochures
eager to explore the mysteries
of Highway Nine.

Dear Ann:

within this grand model of the sign

i shall live a little longer than God
hoping the bad infinity's inside of
jogging to the end of a grey relationship.

Yours Desperate.

Dear Desperate

In case of an exit
please use the nearest emergency.

Envoi

But it is not our wish to reproduce
     ourselves through you
         the reader,
nor to reassure you that these words are true
or where the line breaks   there is a meaning
ſtabilized   by that news
speech is   assuring you
our plans are ſtill the same
as when we met original in formal theory
by the fridge on the ſtreetcar
     beneath some baggage of your satisfaċtions.

Over this our patience supports you
     beneath the topical tuck
which is basic
         to a sand ruse for writing through
these intervals between
         our disagreeable achievements
signed in the triplicate ſtage of the plainer ſtyle
moved on
(not much of it)   to where
the shade from the ilex soaks
the officer in charge

     by the oċtagon

         in auguſt

more or less.

Future Indicative

A flag effects meaning.   But somehow
purpose is closed.

Go into the garden through
each dictionary definition of plot.

The key still trembles from
this single ignition.   Pathetic

as fallacies,   the pains in
the lower back

of politics as fate.
Come to Paris.

The Self meets thought as thought
becomes a thinking other.

Truth
as a neighbourhood.

Pin Yin

The need is since
resemblance hangs passive
edge links a function
to their radicals a phase replacement by distinction of

delinquency
which they describe as absolute
whereas the drip is understood a topic
of the tap but river
total basis thus to sail is
to come back to
peacock net catch stockpile influence in pictures of

a type of withering demand
when quite alike
the aperture pooled harvests fill
the right slide into nouns which specify
disease is in a change from logics
of foundation clue being
conventionally day across the box state only in the helix of

portmanteau shapings
predicate descent before the inches
pull a plural corpse
against the frequency attested as a sample of

'my mouth is earth's scholar'
the heart hands literature a door
means 'moons' to say 'too smooth'
agronomy not born of melon ripening
to bean what walks will usually
be held with little substance relative to meanings of

the flesh
required official as the self
locks up a chest completes
pronunciation local dialect per square
mile everything by water power to sleep a line
machined aquatic to the sorted sequence held in lieu of

idioms
the recent baker's grins
a virulence links cause to agent sausage
encapsulates possessive pork shown true
whereby to rain is
chosen everywhere occasion by analogy
the componential in arrears because a dalliance through form of

finger pushed effects stands bold
supposes phasing change not sense
to numerals the disambiguated geese
all ditto signs of january genuine
as in 'to parse' will differentiate
the workers from their colleagues' known dilemma of

a tightrope value modified
to have no motion
mobile cows in stable gatherings
collect a daytime context
mutton independent of the means set up by study of

the rain's coast over detail
to relations in
i have a cloud and everyday a use comes
tangled in a sequence cooked
rice tentative a thousand shops
the other fixed a figurative wheel extension of

'my face is not up' the medium
is whiſtling at ſtudy speculation
grounds in not begun 'my finish in
a speech-aét tending song'
the band's reality thus swing
through motion verb in error fixed
because one cannot buy the done in times of

plenitude a colour blood
goes up with clothing from the weſt
it ſtands itinerary element in door
juſt opening mnemonics to a type of

shawm.

DOCUMENTS

Transitions to the Beast

This slender booklet from 1970 gathers some early attempts at a post-semiotic poetry. Emerging out of long and lively conversations with bpNichol, the book aimed 'ambitiously' (read 'hubristically') at rectifying the aporia I sensed in both the theory and productions of Semiotic Poetry that arose in São Paulo, Brazil, circa 1964 in the work of Luiz Angelo Pinto and Decio Pignatari. The original afterword to the *Transitions* is reprinted for its documentary relevance. In retrospect I'm still supportive of the desire for an absolute liberation from the word and the retention of a reading competence in the face of a text without words. That was the felt power of the negative at the time. Visually the *Transitions* develop two early proclivities: a movement into clear, intersecting and overlapping geometrical patterns (that now seem to have a nostalgically constructivist air to them), and into a more animated composition of three-dimensional forms whose power derives from the replacement of syntax and articulation by impact, collision and a zoomorphic line of flight. The latter became realized in vast numbers of largely unpublished animated letter shapes (predominantly A and E) composed at the same time as Nichol's own prolific meditations on and encounters with the letter H. I now read my own desire at the time as similar to his: to convey a base sense of the materiality of the letter as 'mass times movement', perhaps even as a living form that hints at that complex delerial notion of 'the life and history of language'. Back to the fiction of Fielding, Smollett and Sterne? Or is it Joyce's *Finnegans Wake* that hovers as the covering cherub here?

Included below are comments I made about the work to bp Nichol in a 1987 interview – see *Open Letter* 6:9 (Fall) 1987.

My introduction to the term 'semiotic' didn't come through the normal, the 'expected' channels – Umberto Eco, Thomas Sebeok, et al., but through the Brazilian concrete poet Decio Pigniatari, who himself adopted the term directly from C. S. Peirce.

In the mid-sixties Pigniatari & others developed the 'semiotic poem', a kind of hybridization of an urban semantic instrumentality (road, signs, traffic signals, for instance)

& the more transgressive abandonment of conventional supports for transactions of meaning. The [resulting] poems were sequences of geometrical shapes which were assigned a specific verbal value (a square might = 'woman'; a triangle = 'man'; the intersection of the two [might be assigned] the meaning 'child'.) What excited me instantly about the semiotic poem was the potential for non-verbal progressions allowing a type of reading to develop that was much closer to the classic category of 'seeing'. What I quickly [realized] as problematic was the ultimate regression back to verbal meaning as a final product. We [myself and bp Nichol] arrived back at the meanings produced by a reading but through a methodology of non-verbal pattern recognitions. That's when you [bp] and I developed the post-semiotic poem in which the lexical key was jettisoned and the poem functioned as a totally unprescribed, or open, form, as a sort of eventist movement of shapes to which a mean could be assigned by the reader*. Already I was ruminating on the power relationship embodied in the reader-writer figuration, desiring increasingly a shift of control from writer to reader. The possibility of a credible psychoaesthetics that would be founded on the glissando between seeing and reading has always fascinated me.

The semiotic poem did generate a parodic response in John Furnival's 'semi-idiotic' poems.

---

* I developed a variant of the semiotic poem in a series of texts termed lexical transformations, in which specific words would be reassigned a new, often phrasal value. Such as 'blue' = 'you can't see the wood for the trees.' Examples of this form will be included in volume two of this selection.

The following is from a letter I wrote to Caroline Bayard (23 January 1980) in response to a section of her work in progress, *The New Poetics in Canada and Quebec*, entitled 'Concrete Theory in English Canada' and containing her interpretation of *Transitions*.

what you say in that section i really like. the perspective vis a vis the brazilian semioticist is very important. what you might like to mention is subsequent developments in europe and south america subsequent to TRANSITIONS *most notably the emergence of the* PROCESS POEM *in czechoslovakia and (i think?) argentina which similarly eliminated lexical keys. the whole emergence is very complex: a) we don't know what is actual conscious influence and what is cultural convergence. i tend to feel that most is cultural convergence ... what you should emphasize however is the political aspect of that work which has always been an important area for me. most important is the switch and reconstitution of the semiotic circuit occasioned by the post-semiotic text which puts the reader in the fresh role as an active producer of signs [correct that to signification] rather than a decipherer or consumer of messages. to consider what you term canadian concrete theory (i truly don't like the phrase and feel it more misrepresenting than helpful) from the angle of a sociology of readership might be most interesting. for involved in the post-semiotic idea (and conscious to my mind at the time) was a contribution to the destruction of writing itself. we didn't have derrida and the concept of deconstruction at that time but i was conscious of creating a text structured upon a partial adoption of the* SIGN: *strategically abandoning the signified and constructing a network of non-linear signifiers that had the additional potential of transgressing currently established categorical boundaries. for instance: the pertinent issue that* TRANSITIONS *might raise of an intra-psychological placement between the two (separate) regions of seeing and reading (instigating such further questions as how does one see a reading and would that be any different from reading your seeing). but the shift in* TRANSITIONS *is very important from a communicative basis for the text to a non-*

communicative base; a base from which the relevant epistemological question becomes NOT *how do we decipher this meaning but how is meaning to be produced:* THE POLITICAL ECONOMY OF THE SIGN.

aftermath [original afterword to *Transitions*]

to the beast are for me transitional pieces moving towards a hand drawn set of visual conventions that have their roots both in semiotic poetry & in the comic strip. the semiotic or code poem (invented round about 1964 by the brazilians pigniatari & pinto) uses a language of visual signs designed & constructed to suit the individual desires of the poet & the needs that he, as linguistic designer, assumes for the poem on that particular occasion of construction.

the striking impulse behind this type of poem is both alinear & nonlexical – the desire to expand language beyond the single limited form of verbal expression. however the abandoning of traditional verbal form in favour of a set of visual signs anchored in functionality & pragmatism has not produced a truly verbally liberated poetry for the ultimate recourse to a lexical key in order to supply a verbal definition of the signs (which most semioticists apparently feel necessary) radically neutralizes, if not destroys, all the professed nonlexical directions of this form of poetry. in addition to the felt necessity for a lexical support most code poems that i have seen assume the form of a successive order of coded states using in fact an episodic technique on the visual sign level to express changes in state & preserving thereby that sense of arrested flow characteristic of linear based language.

the earlier poems in this book are experiments around these two problems e.g. in the use of 3 dimensional syntax & the general complications of the visual level of information to a point beyond the one to one relationship of key & sign. the desire was to attain a cool code (low definition) a language of immediate and tight visual impact with no spatial separation to assist poetic movement creative involvement on the readers part & the expression of single complex relationships in preference to the presentation of developing content (i'm thinking of such secular relationships as man to language man is a world & the word as a world.)

most of the poems are built from the single letter E which functions in the series as a single nonspecific sign or potential code (sometimes using other letters such as K & M but for the same purpose, sometimes a combination of more than one but for the same purpose) the manipulation of perspective and shape of the letter is the basic syntactic tool relating the letters to letters & elements of the single letter to other elements. the later poems deepen the search for visual conventions to help extend my own range of expression & especially to carry suggestions of the weight & bulk of language (language as weight linguistic weight as history not the history of language but the language of history as bpNichol once said). that this may oppose many features of semiotic poetry doesn't worry me, the semiotic form acted only as the initial impulse to search for a nonlexical sign language. increasingly (& this in spite of this afterblurb) i'm feeling the need for a more rawly human & a less technocratic approach to the borderblur for a greater degree of idiosyncratic expression as far as this helps present the poet's own perceptual system, entry in short of more personal feeling & due attention to our more simplistic responses to & in front of language.

at the time of writing i felt strongly the need to present my own personal & still emerging system. to achieve this end with any degree of satisfaction involved me in a return to the hand as the basis of composition & in return to the line as distinct from linearity & into manual construction as a part step in bringing poetry back to the body where it truly belongs.

transitions to the beast have an increasingly diminishing relevance to my current spaces; they have served a function & that's why they are being published now in the hope that they might still have relevance to others.

not so depressed as me

smcc 1970

Broken Mandala

I can't improve on my earlier comments on this work published in *Open Letter* 6:9 (Fall) 1987, some of which I repeat here almost verbatim. Suffice to add that during my graduate research in 1969 (a little before composing the *Mandala*) I came across Christopher Smart's famous theory of poetic impression. (It occurs in the Preface to Smart's translations of Horace, 1767, and in a different, more striking version, in his *Jubilate Agno*): 'Impression, then, is a talent or gift of Almighty God, by which a Genius is empowered to throw an emphasis upon a word or sentence in such wise, that it cannot escape any reader of sheer, and true critical sagacity.' The articulation of the impress onto the mechanics of type manufacture and type-setting is brought out forcibly in this passage from the *Jubilate Agno*: 'For my talent is to give an impression upon words by punching, that when the reader casts his eye upon 'em, he takes up the image from the mould wch I have made.' At the time *Broken Mandala* was composed I was working in the Office of the Queen's Printer (my one and only royal appointment!) and the desire to capture the force of sheer imprint was certainly a major concern in the series. Imprint as it registers as a gestural, manual trace, a hand-print impressed upon language. Ron Silliman would subsequently urge the return to a more gestural poetics. This concern with the gestural is also present in the many hand drawn visual poems I did around this time (see some in the *Transitions to the Beast* section) and carried over into my text-sound and sound performance work, both solo and with the Four Horsemen.

The *Mandala* 'breaks' in the sense that the circle transforms into a rayonistic syntax. A replacement of the circle (and all its symbolic, emblematic burden) by a repeated rubber stamp whose message is repetitive and mundane. The work was a kind of apocalyptic perspective induced upon cliché, archetype and dominant cultural discourse. There is also the desire to confound the psycho-social boundaries that would divide a 'reading' from a 'seeing'. This marginality has been a constant concern in all my visual texts. I suppose there is present a kind of theological code. The eye in the centre of one of the texts is incredibly hieroglyphic. Yet my concern was entirely with writing and the various partitionings of a scriptive surface. Hence, a grammatological rather than a theological concern …

There was also in *Broken Mandala* a cinematic concern. I composed this work in the early seventies when I was developing an intereſt in Gertrude Stein's writings and her application of the cinematic frame to language. I was reading too the Danish linguiſt Louis Hjelmslev and became intrigued by his notion of the 'kineme': a linguiſtic unit considered as a unit of movement. Movement, slippage and collision were all key concepts in my composition of the pieces in *Broken Mandala*. [This intereſt in the dynamic movement of linguiſtic signs developed further in my subsequent research into, and application of, both the paragram, or 'moving' gram and the clinamen, or minimum atomic swerve.]

There is also the concern with a contemporary reappropriation of pictorial, ideogrammatic and hieroglyphic forms. I saw this as both a development from, and eventually an alternative to, Pound's notion [via Fenollosa] of the Chinese written character. It was intensely 'semiotic' work, and intensely political too. The politics did not inhere in content but in the disposition of the language as a pure, graphic materiality, which I saw as a defetishizing [ſtrategy].

Broken Mandala emerged during an obsessive preoccupation with violence in my writing; a violence that was not the object of a content but rather demonſtrative, inherent and active [enactual?] within the material subſtance of the language. (The concept of a 'materialiſt poetics' was very important in my thinking around this time, when i rejected idealiſt notions of language, meaning and truth-production. I discarded image, description [discredited since Williams, Olson and Creeley] and had begun to focus on language almoſt as paint, as pure graphic subſtance.)

A singular weakness of *Broken Mandala* is the failure to move this clash of linguiſtic dispositions (material sign on the one hand and idealiſt referentiality on the other) beyond a ſtaged representation and into an effective form of immanent critique. So the work remains theatrical and on that account ſtill of a representational nature. The work ſtill supports a fetishized perception & does not eliminate the 'gaze' as an optical transaction across a diſtance between an unproblematic text & an unproblematic self.

'Ow's "Waif"

These poems arose from some earlier attempts at applying the process of translation to poems in the same language as part of a wider attempt to create a satisfying form of synthetic composition. These early experiments were reported and discussed in some depth in Report 1 of The Toronto Research Group (TRG) published in *Open Letter* (2nd Series No. 4, Spring 1973). This type of composition permits the writer a near to total separation of form from content, the entire 'borrowing' of content as a prepared word-supply (a 'supply-text') and a creative concentration on the invention of the poems' forms as verbal fields free of presupposed or prerequisite rule structures of grammar and syntax.

Each poem, then, results from a calculated action upon a specific word-source or 'supply-text'. This text functions as the total available language system for the poem – a specific limitation of vocabulary. The supply-texts were chosen at random from books, articles, magazines, newspapers, etc. that had happened to be close by me at the times I felt the urge to write: *Newton's Optics* 1705 ed., an Evelyn Waugh biography of Edmund Campion, Susanna Moodie's *Roughing it in the Bush*, a trigonometry textbook, Jacques Maritain's *Creative Intuition in Art and Poetry*, E.A. Poe's *The Poetic Principle* and John Cage's *Notebook: 'A Year from Monday'*. For the 'Ten Portraits' I used as supply-texts ten separate and randomly chosen phrases from a transcribed interview with some N.Y. prostitutes.

The method of invention involved some systematic-chance structures to determine such things as word frequency, word recurrence, patterns of sonorities and termination of breath lines. At other times numerical determinants were used for word selection, other times word selection was a careful conscious choice, other times vertical and diagonal readings of the supply-text and/or random (closed eye) word selection to arrive at a final poem. The operating analogy in many cases was cubism: the process of fragmentation and reconstitution of a known thing in a fresh form. The poems are best read aloud.

smcc

toronto, may 1973

Dr Sadhu's Muffins:
Note on the Method of Composition

These poems were an attempt to produce texts which directly presented language-material without the intrusion of my own consciousness. This in itself formed part of a wider attempt to write poems that were mutually revelatory to both reader and writer. As such my concern was less with presenting statements and ideas and more with the accurate transcription of a pure perceptual process of the writer functioning as reader.

To achieve this I used numerous chance and random techniques to assist me in word selection and partial syntactic structuring to a degree such as would keep me excluded from the content part of the compositions. In most cases the word selection for any one poem was determined by a non-intentional reading among a supply-text chosen at random from whatever happened to be on my desk when I was working: a *Concise Oxford Dictionary*, the works of Shakespeare, the poems of John Donne, an *I-Ching*, newspapers, *Life* magazine, *Scientific American*, abandoned drafts of several of my own poems, etc. Any supply-text of this kind became the maximum available vocabulary for any one piece and operated as a source of linguistic material capable of finding release into 'my' poem along one of several reading paths. In choosing to write my own reading in this way the poems became transcriptions of the movement of the moment under actual observation. They graphed a treatment of my own reading experience as a kind of seeing (Pound's sense of translation) graphing a reflex activity of my own eyes from off an arbitrary verbal surface, freezing a random sequence of words into a meaningful form.

As a poet I took responsibility for the page but not necessarily for everything that found its way onto the page. What I did was set up the sufficient conditions for any open field to form into which a word could find its own way settling in its own syntactic space and thereby determining the meaning of that space. This type of acausal composition involves the writer and the reader as coinitiators of a language event that both begins and ends as a reading experience thus, in a sense, eliminating all 'writing' from the writing and negating the functional stance of the writer as anything more than a seer of his own reading.

Having no responsibility whatsoever for the lexical material I found that I could concentrate exclusively on the invention of form – on the realignment of discrete semantic units into either open or closed fields of independent energy and image. What I found was the less care and responsibility I took with any formal matters the more complex and absorbing were the poems that resulted.

The 'Anamorphoses' were attempts to 'describe out of definition', to transform a comprehension into a perception, the known thing into the thing seen, by having a text generate itself out of the dictionary definition of its title. 'The Redwood Suite' was first performed as a simultaneous reading at Carleton University in October of 1973.

smcc, toronto, april 1974

Carnival

The following excerpts were published as prefatory matter in the firSt edition of *Carnival : The FirSt Panel.*

the duality between poetry and prose can no longer be maintained
the duality between form and content can no longer be maintained
thus for the modern writer form will have a direClly spiritual
meaning
it will not describe events
it will not describe at all
but ESCRIBE
it will recreate in the world the common meaning of events

– de Stijl manifeSto 1920

Carnival: The Second Panel has a short quotation and a longer IntroduCtion, faithfully reprinted here in all its rebarbative pretentiousness:

> *If the Revolution could be spoken, it would be only with a*
> *discourse that cannot assume a coherent position of truth,*
> *with a series of contradiClory voices that cannot know*
> *themselves, which do not conSlitute a point of view, which*
> *repeat themselves and fall apart, only in order to be able to*
> *begin again.*

– Ann Smock & Phyllis Zuckerman

Introduction

Carnival is planned as a multi-panel language environment, conStruCted largely on a typewriter and designed ultimately to put the reader, as perceptual participant, within the centre of his language.

The roots of *Carnival* go beyond concretism (specifically that particular branch of concrete poetry termed the 'typeStraCt' or abStraCt typewriter art) to labyrinth and mandala, and all related archetypal forms that emphasize the use of the visual qualities of language to defend a sacred centre. Pound's vorticism also forms part of the grid of influences, and on one level at least, *Carnival* can be seen as an attempt to abstract, concretize and expand Pound's concept of the images as the circular pull of an intellectual and emotional energy. Above all it is a structure of strategic counter-communication designed to draw a reader inward to a locus where text surrounds her. Language units are placed in visible conflict, in patterns of defective messages, creating a semantic texture by shaping an interference within the clear line of statement.

Panel Two is largely an expression of language emerging into conflict and internecine statement conveyed in the variety of mechanical means of expression that's employed. It was predicated on a felt implication in Saussure's assertion that language is differential and oppositive at base. Having discovered, explored, and tested the parameters of the typewriter in *The First Panel*, *The Second Panel* places the typed mode in agonistic relation with other forms of scription: xerography, xerography within xerography (i.e. metaxerography and disintegrative seriality), electrostasis, rubber stamp, tissue texts, hand-lettering and stencil. The compositional problem was in finding a form large enough to accommodate these conflicts and what arose as a solution was the interlocking single page to form a sixteen unit panel with the offset book format (to be abandoned in the process of assembling the panel) constituting the final stage in the process of transmutating the scription. The second panel, then, applies a translative process to language's most physical and concrete levels: script and grapheme.

Two phrases seemed to haunt me during the five years of composition. One, that form 'is the only possible thing' – a phrase, I think, that either echoes or cribs a line in Paul Blackburn's *Journals*. The other was Pound's lines in 'Canto cxvi':

to 'see again,'
the verb is 'see,' not 'walk on'

a profound phrase which I take to be Pound's ultimate stand in support of static, synchronic vista (Dante) as opposed to the dynamic line of processual flow. Dante climbed, in the *Paradiso*, out of narrative into a non-narrative summation of the story line –

as if art struggles to distance that which threatens it in closest proximity: language itself. *Carnival* is product and machine, not process; though its creation be a calenture to me, it must stand objective as distancing and isolating of the language experience. The thrust is geomantic – realignment of speech, like earth, for purposes of intelligible access to its neglected qualities of immanence and non-reference. It is language presented as direct physical impact, constructed as a peak, at first to stand on and look down on from the privilege of distance onto language as something separate from you. Taken this way – as the 'seen thing' – its conflicts and contradictions are accommodated in a form based more on the free flight of its particulars than on a rigid component control. But *Carnival* is also peak to descend from into language. The panel when 'seen' is 'all language at a distance'; the panel when read is entered, and offers the reader the experience of non-narrative language. There are no clues to passage for the reader other than the one phrase of Kung's: 'make it new', move freely, as the language itself moves, along one and more of the countless reading paths available, through zones of familiar sense into the opaque regions of the unintelligible, and then out again to savour the collision of the language groupings. Against the melodic line which is narative I work with semantic patchwork, blocks of truncated sense that overlap, converge, collide without transition as the sum total of language games within our many universes of discourse.

1975

The following reflections are taken from a 1998 interview with Peter Jaeger published in *Open Letter* 10. 4 (Fall) 1998:

> Carnival *is closer to cartography, to a diagram or topological surface than a poem or 'text' – (it's also been referred to as typewriter art and a typestract panel). The shape of the panel resulted from a technique of masking (i.e. a sheet of blank paper cut into a particular shape is placed over a normal rectangular sheet and typing is continuous over both surfaces, thus producing a patterned blank space on the lower sheet).* Carnival *eschews any general left-right*

orientation that stabilizes linear terrains, but the resulting textual space is less labyrinthine or rhizomatic than striated, layered with fault lines, fissures, blocks, apertures, dead-ends, blocked linearities, boundaries, textual hollows, semanticgeodes, overprints, concretions, excretions. *All of this serves to provide simultaneously a map and the territory mapped, a geology, and a field in which continuous linear syntax is replaced with detours and continuations, propelling the reader-traveller into morphings and movements. At the time of its composition, I conceived* Carnival *as a calculated intervention into the material stakes of poetics. The hegemonic weight (in what Don Allen dubbed the New American Poetry) of Olson's triple theories of proprioception, projective verse and human universe were extremely powerful during my formative years as a writer in North America, and* Carnival, *in part, registers a personal attempt to repudiate one of Olson's theories and to extend another. Respectively: 1) the repudiation of a breath-based poetics; 2) the extension of the typewriter beyond Olson's own estimation of its abilities (to provide a precise notation of breathing) into a more 'expressionistic' as well as cartographic instrument, approaching the typewriter less as a notational device than a form of saxophone.*

As regards its constructive materials I tried consciously to expand the repertoire of different methods of 'imprint'. As well as a typewriter, I used manual marking, xerographic modification of early wet-feed electrostatic reproductions, rubber stamps and typed text on tissue paper subsequently crumpled and xeroxed, deliberate photographic disintegration by lessening contrast and repetitive copyings of copies, manual reconstruction of some of these disintegrations, random ink effects created by carbon paper passed back and forth over a blank sheet of paper and dragged through a loose typewriter carriage, etc. Although published as a two colour work, in the original I used four different colours of ribbon. (I thought of this hybrid way of composing, this composition by heterogenous means, as analogous to John Cage's prepared pianos.) Much collage material is incorporated alongside both spontaneous and calculated writing, and compositionally designed so that 'revision' and 'correction' were impossible. To 'revise' would be equivalent to either abandoning or adding to the work.

Is it a book or is it typewriter art? Can it be both? Jerome McGann distinguishes between nonnarrative and antinarrative. Carnival *deliberately problematizes the simple distinction between seeing and reading and offers itself for both distant viewing and close reading – a double dimension and double possibility that's important. Moreover, it requires a performative gesture on the reader's part. In its initial state,* Carnival *is a 'book' i.e. a bound sequence of regular pages. Each page is perforated at the top and the panel-object can only be realized by the willful destruction of the book-object. As an 'unripped book'* Carnival *remains merely a virtual panel, whereas a mounted panel is a 'book destroyed'.* The Second Panel *of* Carnival *predictably follows an earlier, strictly typographic, panel, both of which were designed as part of a larger environmental assemblage to cover floors, walls and ceilings, creating an axonometric syntax to convert text and map into architectural dwelling. Both a third panel and the project in general were abandoned. Long out of print and off walls, both panels are available today in an electronic version housed at www.chbooks.com.*

Postcards of the assembled *Carnival* panels showing their original colours have been tipped in to the first edition of this book.

Every Way Oakly

This manuscript is a draft of translations from Gertrude Stein's *Tender Buttons*. It presents initial investigations in the concept of homolinguistic translation (translation within the same language) and the use of such a type of translation to generate contentually new texts that, nonetheless, obey certain of the basic tenets of translation (the passage from a source to a target language and the preservation, in that passage, of some trace of the source elements.)

In *Tender Buttons* Stein composed a series of cubist still lifes in words. In developing her cubist descriptions Stein found it crucial to include the peripheralities of her own viewpoint and a description of the subjective perceptual experience itself within, and as part of, the actual description of the object. In the present translation this cubist perceptual method has been preserved and Stein's method of observation and description has become my method of reading and translating. As such, these poems can be seen as a recontextualization of Stein's perceptual methodology within the linguistic discipline of translation. The source texts (Stein's original pieces) become textual still lifes placed under the rigour of translational observation so as to generate their target texts along the lines of allusive reference and connotational structures and possibilities.

It's suggested that a reader have handy a copy of Stein's original for comparison. Ideally, get a friend to read the translations aloud to you whilst you, simultaneously, read the original *Tender Buttons*.

smcc, 30 december 1977

note: from the original texts emerged points of replacement – viz. certain words which would be capable of replacement by synonyms or synonymously inspired associations. These points constitute the translated nuclei – the connecting verbal material being freely supplied by the translator.

Shifters: a note

shifters i.e. overlappings of message and code. indices (Peirce). non-commital formal indicators (Heidegger). *'Dasein*-designations'. ego-centric particulars (Russell).

a true subject is a barred subject.

shifters shift within a topography and topology of text where every 'i' is a 'here' every 'you' a 'there'. poems then of openness and closure. semiotic bars and semiotic centres unfolding as tests of their own meanings.

both the discourse of self and 'de Alio in oratione'.

shifters. producers of such interrogations as:
how is meaning created?
when is a then a there?
what is tense, time and interlocution?

frames in which he and she can never reflect
that instance of discourse they are a part of.

apart from.
remnants. externalities.

instants out of discourse.

steve mccaffery
june 1976

Shifters

In part *Shifters* was a personal attempt to come to terms with the problematics of a lyric subject, and, more generally, the place of the self within writing. A 'shifter' is a term from linguistics popularized by both Jesperson and Jakobson but perhaps most concisely defined by Emile Benveniste. Shifters include all pronouns and indicators and mark actual 'instances of discourse'. An I refers to 'the individual individual who utters the present instance of discourse containing the linguistic instance I'. Here was theorized the kinds of linkage slippage and movement that I've always found attractive, but more importantly at the time it showed me the essential nature of 'I' as an empty sign, a fundamental negativity and potentiality to be filled, occupied and then abandoned. At the time of composing *Shifters* I was convinced of the essentially spatial notion of locutory identity; that 'I' and 'You' mark less an identity than a position and this led me into examining the numerous topologies of 'self' in writing. The work too was pivotal in my growing awareness of writing's 'thanato-practic' nature; that writing links more to an economy of death and absence than one of vitality and presence. Writing renders the writer dispensible; the writer becomes dead to the work on its completion.

A Note on *Intimate Distortions*

This book might be considered a contribution to homolinguistic translation, adopting as it does a translation method called 'allusive referential'. I developed the method through the mid-1970s in correspondence and samples with Dick Higgins. We had earlier collaborated with bpNichol on *Six Fillious* (Milwaukee: Membrane Press, 1978): a three-way translation of Robert Filliou's *14 chansons et 1 charade* (Stuttgart: edition hansjorg mayer, 1968) and the earlier translations by Fluxus artists Diter Rot (into German) and George Brecht (into English.) Unlike homophonic translation, allusive referential involves an associative-semantic method, the rule for translation being to develop any number of suggestions and connotations latent in words and phrases found in the source text. Higgins and I saw allusive referential as a facet of a wider notion we termed 'Creative Misunderstanding'. *Intimate Distortions* used as its source text the Mary Barnard translation of Sappho (University of California Press, 1958).

Evoba

Evoba is dialogic and equally parasitic, reversing the normal poles of primary and secondary discourse in which philosophy engages poetry. The late Elaine Vitale supplied the following comments that appeared on the book's back cover. '*Evoba* (pronounced "vubba") unfolds a fascinating poetic response cum antidote to Wittgenstein's *Philosophical Investigations*. McCaffery's new-old work exemplifies with disturbing lucidity the way one text can read another and plunge reader and writer alike across discursive difference into the paradoxical space between two meanings'. An opening epigraph to this work may also be relevant in this documentary section: 'If the aim of philosophy is, as Wittgenstein claims, to show the fly the way out of the fly bottle, then the aim of poetry is to convince the bottle that there is no fly'.

The Scenarios

The Scenarios are best considered as short movie scripts or inter-
media texts falling between the categories of motion picture and
poem. The artistic deal is this: as author i'll provide the film if
you promise to provide your own camera. Alternatively we can
both perform them separately.

1980

Knowledge Never Knew

In contrast to the integrated, discursive prose of the critical essay, the aphorism presents itself as condensed and discontinuous, calling attention to its own lack of context. Showing the humility of the fragment it also resonates the arrogance of the bald assertion. *Knowledge Never Knew*, however, strives to go beyond the aphorism putting into play its splendid isolation with a parallel ghost, mirror phrase or strange attractor. The book takes the form of two bands related across the blank space of each page: an aphoristic lower band, and an upper factual and fictional band relating crystal thought to chronology across an unrelated space. This white space and absence is vital to the textual economy in which void and blank become charged with an an overflow of the non-written. As Deleuze informs, 'The void has never been hostile to the particles which move about in it'. Nonetheless, a thought may link with a neighbouring fact (or lie) connecting in that paradoxical relation Gilles Deleuze calls a 'disjunctive synthesis'. As I commented to bpNichol in 1987, *Knowledge Never Knew* stages 'the proposition as an ideological object and articulates language [onto] both fact, [fiction] and paradox, thereby reflecting the historical that produced it. You might say that it [sets in play] the logical and linguistic forms that make history palpable and manifest'. I now see the book as both architectural and deconstructive. The following is a slightly modified version of part of the book's original jacket copy.

> Knowledge Never Knew *is both a book and not a book. Posing itself as essentially a hundred pages of unthinkable space it brings together and holds apart two threads of discontinuous discourse: the one a series of useless historical facts mixed freely with historical lies, the other a pot pourri of cantilations invoked in the mental shadow of a complete atlas of the paradoxical. These aphorisms, then thought of as condensed ruins, assiduously comment on and cast thought around the key terms of book, performance, writing, philosophy and living.*

The Black Debt: A Note on *Lag*

'Lag' has been contrasted to Ron Silliman's theory and practice of the New Sentence, reducing the units of non-integration from Silliman's sentence down to the phrase. The compositional units of 'Lag' are simple: a phrase partitioned by a comma. It is one of several attempts I've made to use 'critical theory' as a formal model for text generation. In 'Lag' I use Lyotard's theory of 'phrase dispute' as outlined in the beginning of his book *The Differend: Phrases in Dispute* (University of Minnesota Press, 1988). One aspect of his theory of phrase linkage impressed me very forcibly: the paradoxical nature of 'the final phrase'. Phrase economies are endless and resist closure. 'For a phrase to be the last one, another one is needed to declare it, and it is then not the last one' (*The Differend*, p.11). This might explain the vertiginousness movement of 'Lag', despite its formal predictability, as a flood without totality of heterogenous phrase objects emerging and disappearing within a rigid ascetic force of partition and linkage. Of the linkage itself: the phrases that comprise 'Lag' do not connect in order to narrate but to decentre and scatter. Where reference occurs the referent is not a given but an instant to be established and departed. Two other claims of Lyotard were germinal to the poem: 'A phrase, which links and is to be linked, is always a pagus, a border zone where genres of discourse enter into conflict over the mode of linking' (151). 'To save the phrase: extract it from discourses in which it is subjugated and restrained by rules for linking' (68). Phrases 'can obey regimens other than the logical and the cognitive. They can have stakes other than the true' (65). One other concept helped me formulate 'Lag': Gilles Deleuze's notion of becoming. I wanted 'Lag''s incessant rhythm of propulsion, brevity, instant happening and anullment to suggest a constant 'becoming-meaning' and to shift from a 'logic' to a 'physics' and 'kinetics' of reading.

Bibliography

Works by Steve McCaffery excerpted in this text include:

Transitions to the Beast. Toronto: *grOnk* series 6 2&3/
    Ganglia Press, 1970.
CARNIVAL the first panel: 1967–70. Toronto:
    Coach House Press, 1973.*
Broken Mandala. Toronto: *grOnk* IS2/Ganglia Press, 1974.
Dr Sadhu's Muffins. Erin, Ontario: Press Porcépic, 1974.
Horse d'Oeuvres. (With the Four Horsemen.) Don Mills:
    PaperJacks, 1975.
'Ow's "Waif ". Toronto: Coach House Press, 1975.
Shifters. Toronto: *grOnk* IS 6/Ganglia Press, 1976.
CARNIVAL the second panel: 1970–75. Toronto:
    Coach House Press, 1977.*
Crown's Creek. (With Steven Smith.) Toronto/Vancouver:
    Anonbeyond Press, 1978.
Every Way Oakly. Edmonton: Stephen Scobie, 1978.
In England Now That Spring. (With bpNichol.) Toronto:
    Aya Press, 1979.
Intimate Distortions. Erin, Ontario: Porcupine's Quill, 1979.
The Scenarios. Toronto: League of Canadian Poets, 1980.
Knowledge Never Knew. Montréal: Véhicule Press, 1983.
Panopticon. Toronto: blewointmentpress, 1984.
Evoba: The Investigations Meditations 1976–78. Toronto:
    Coach House Press, 1987.
The Black Debt. London, Ontario: Nightwood Editions, 1989.
Theory of Sediment. Vancouver: Talonbooks, 1991.
Modern Reading: Poems 1969–1990. London, England:
    Writers Forum, 1992.
The Cheat of Words. Toronto: ECW Press, 1996.

* images of the assembled *CARNIVAL* panels (including the
two-colour first panel and the unpublished five-colour version of
the second panel) have been produced as postcards to accom-
pany this text.

For a more detailed bibliography of McCaffery's œuvre, see
bpNichol, 'The Annotated, Anecdoted, Beginnings of a Critical
Checklist of the Published Works of Steve McCaffery.' *Open
Letter* 6.9 (fall 1987): 67–92.

Acknowledgements

Thanks to all the editors, publishers and presses who helped these poems and texts firſt see the light of day. Special thanks to Darren Wershler-Henry and Alana Wilcox for their skills, tastes, suggeſtions, vigilance and belief in the produ&tion of this book and to Rick/Simon for the use of the cover image.

Thanks also to the Ontario Arts Council and the Canada Council for their generous support over the years. Moſt recently, this support took the form of a 1998 Canada Council creative writing grant, without which this work could not have been completed.

A Note on the Design

The process of taking selections from the entirety of Steve McCaffery's heterogeneous published works and then attempting to set them all in the same typeface on a uniform page size can only be described as 'procrustean'.

Many of the texts in *Seven Pages Missing* were composed for an 8.5" x 11" page on a manual typewriter, and were set in Courier or some other monospaced font. I have tried to preserve as much of the spacing of the published versions of the poems as possible, and have followed the original page breaks in many cases as well (the most obvious exception is the excerpts from *Evoba*, where the original pages are extremely long). All of the changes to the formatting of published works were made after discussing them with the author, and should be viewed as homolinguistic 'translations' of texts that in most cases have no original ...

The visual works reproduced here were also problematic. Once again, many of the original versions have been lost, but we worked from originals wherever possible. It's usually possible to salvage a line drawing from a reproduction of even indifferent quality, but McCaffery's newspaper collages (such as the Pound poems in *Modern Reading*) did not as fare well because of the high acid content of the paper and the moiré patterns that appear after rescanning a half-tone image. The versions of the visual poems in this book, then, are (relatively) 'noise-free' translations that emphasize graphic form rather than the current condition of the source documents.

Darren Wershler-Henry
December 2000

Typeset in Adobe Caslon
at Coach House Printing on bpNichol Lane, 2000

Edited and designed by Darren Wershler-Henry
Copy edited and proofread by Alana Wilcox
Cover image by Rick/Simon

To read the online version of this text and other titles from
Coach House Books, visit our website:
www.chbooks.com

To add your name to our e-mailing list, write:
mail@chbooks.com

Toll-free:
1 800 376 6360

Coach House Books
401 Huron Street (rear) on bpNichol Lane
Toronto, Ontario
M5S 2G5